THE
GINGER & WHITE
COOKBOOK

THE
GINGER & WHITE
COOKBOOK

Tonia George, Emma Scott, & Nicholas Scott

Photography by Jenny Zarins

Mitchell Beazley

THE AUTHORS

Tonia George worked as a food stylist for 10 years and as food editor on the highly acclaimed British magazine *Waitrose Food Illustrated*. She is the author of several cookbooks, including *Things on Toast* (she is a self-confessed toast addict) and *A Perfect Start*. Her work has appeared in numerous publications, including *Living etc.*, *Red* magazine, U.S. *Food and Wine*, and the British *Guardian Weekend* magazine.

Nicholas and Emma Scott have forged successful careers in the restaurant and events sector in both London and Sydney, Australia. Emma has previously worked at the acclaimed British restaurant St John and Terence Conran's Quaglino's and also catered events, including the Wimbledon Tennis Championships. Nick, originally from New Zealand, has worked for some of the top eateries in Sydney and was astounded by the lack of good coffee shops in London. Together, he and Emma ran a consultancy for restaurant owners, which took them all around the world, including to Beijing in the run-up to the Beijing 2008 Olympic Games.

Note: This book contains some dishes made with raw or lightly cooked eggs. It is prudent for more vulnerable people, such as pregnant and nursing mothers, people with weakened immune systems, the elderly, babies, and young children to avoid dishes made with uncooked or lightly cooked eggs.

Ginger & White: The Cookbook
by Tonia George, Emma Scott, & Nicholas Scott

First published in Great Britain in 2014
by Mitchell Beazley, an imprint of
Octopus Publishing Group Limited,
Endeavour House, 189 Shaftesbury Avenue,
London WC2H 8JY
www.octopusbooks.co.uk

An Hachette UK Company
www.hachette.co.uk

Distributed in the US by Hachette Book Group USA,
237 Park Avenue, New York, NY 10017, USA

Distributed in Canada by Canadian Manda Group,
165 Dufferin Street, Toronto, Ontario, Canada M6K 3H6

ISBN: 978 1 84533 901 2

Set in Roswell Four and Tribute.

Printed and bound in China.

Photographer: Jenny Zarins
Food Stylist: Tonia George
Props Stylist: Tabitha Hawkins
Illustrator: Abigail Read

Publisher: Alison Starling
Art Director: Jonathan Christie
Senior Art Editor: Juliette Norsworthy
Senior Editor: Leanne Bryan
Assistant Designer: Grace Helmer
Copyeditor: Trish Burgess
Proofreader: Salima Hirani
Indexer: Hilary Bird
Senior Production Manager: Katherine Hockley

CONTENTS

Introduction

We opened the doors of Ginger & White on a sunny Tuesday in July 2009. It was not the best timing: Emma and Nick were juggling life with a six-month-old baby girl and Tonia was eight months pregnant. Without the budget for an architect, we designed the café ourselves using a ruler and tape measure. We can remember measuring the gap in the counter and toying with how tight we could make it to maximize our minuscule pip-squeak of a kitchen. Then Nick turned to Tonia and ran the tape measure across her baby bump to check that she could still fit through the gap, and that was that: decision made!

This scene pretty much sums up the ad hoc beginnings of Ginger & White. The early days were interspersed with births and babies, but there was also the sad loss of Emma's mom, Jan, a couple of weeks before the opening. So although we dutifully crunched the numbers, most of the time we threw out the rule book and made decisions with our hearts. And one of these was that Ginger & White should have the feel of a family business. There would be no corporate coffee shop formula for us. Our place would be like an extension of Tonia's kitchen and of Nick and Emma's home, with food lovingly

cooked and shared around a communal dining table or on a coffee table in front of a comfy leather sofa. This was to be a place for sharing food, conversation, and laughter.

In our opinion, the café scene in London was in a sorry state and a long way behind that of New Zealand and Australia. It consisted mostly of American-style coffee chains pumping out what they called "real coffee expertly made by baristas," but that we thought would be better described as "frothy pints of milky nothingness." Our coffee was definitely real, but how could we describe it in a way that

distinguished it from the chain-produced product? We eventually came up with, "We *don't* do Grande!" which we hoped would tell our customers that we took coffee seriously enough not to drown it in lukewarm milk.

We talked and talked for months about the perfect café, stitching together the best parts from the antipodean café scene, but desperately wanting to keep a flavor of the traditional British café. So we stood by classics such as the bacon sandwich and baked beans on toast, though our beans were braised with smoked paprika and sweetened with molasses

instead of being poured from a tin. Similarly, the bacon we used came from free-range Blythburgh pigs and the ketchup was a spicy sauce from Wiltshire. We knew that using artisan produce from farmers' markets was going to reduce our profit margin, but we couldn't bring ourselves to go down the well-trodden road of using big, faceless, and much cheaper catering suppliers.

Having decided on the ethos of our café, we now needed to find the perfect corner of London for it. Easier said than done. We looked at countless potential sites, many of which were soulless. One kabob takeout had a basement of bunk beds and more people than you would think could possibly fit in it. And then we came across Chaiwalla, a little chai tea room tucked down a pedestrianized side street in leafy Hampstead, north London. The locals had not quite taken to the idea of drinking chai from terra-cotta cups while perching on Bollywood-style ottomans and then smashing the cups outside, so the owner was selling. We knew it was perfect for us right away.

Once up and running, Ginger & White was quickly packed with customers who all

became part of the family. From tiny toddlers to octogenarians, everyone loved dunking toast "soldiers" into soft-boiled eggs decorated with little woolly hats.

And it is to all our wonderful customers, who have taken us into their hearts, that we dedicate this book; and to our loyal staff, who often feel to us like an excited brood of teenage offspring; and, of course, to our own little munchkins, who are always willing and eager to help when cakes need to be tasted. Thank you also to the grandmas who have knitted our egg cozies or shared trusted family recipes, and to our littlest customers, whom we have nurtured with many a babyccino, fish stick sandwich, and dippy egg.

We want to share this collection of recipes with the entire extended Ginger & White family. Unlike some "proper" chef cookbooks that need to be tweaked in order to be usable in the domestic kitchen, this one consists of dishes that can genuinely be made at home— all the way from our homes to yours—to give you loads of enjoyment with lashings of laughter and fun.

Breakfast & brunch

How to make great coffee

Making great coffee is almost a culinary art. The secret, of course, is to start with great ingredients. At G&W, we use freshly roasted beans that are bagged and then stored for 7–10 days before opening. After that, we grind only what is needed—and we recommend that you do the same, whether it's for an espresso machine, a stove-top percolator, or a standard drip-filter coffeepot.

1. Getting the beans

There are two ways to get your hands on great beans: walk into your closest independent coffee bar or shop, which may actually roast on the premises, or go online and subscribe to one of the boutique roasters. Top of our list is Square Mile Coffee Roasters, whom we've used since day one. However, other notable suppliers include Carvetii, Climpson & Sons, Caravan, Volcano Coffee Works, and Ozone.

2. Grinding the beans

If you are lucky enough to have an espresso machine at home, you will need to grind your beans very finely. They should be a little coarser for a stove-top coffeepot and quite coarse for a French press or drip filter. There are excellent hand grinders now available or you can splash out on an electric grinder, but try to avoid using a spice grinder, as it can give very uneven results.

3. Tamping

Let's assume you have an espresso machine: place freshly ground coffee in the basket of your portafilter, then tamp firmly and evenly (preferably with a tamper) until the coffee pushes back. This produces a firm "puck" of grounds for extraction. A nicely weighted tamper feels great in the hand and is worth the investment.

4. Pulling the shot

A good double espresso (about 1 fl. oz.) should take 27–30 seconds to extract. Any longer and the coffee might taste watery and sour; any less and the coffee will be missing all the wonderful caramel and fruity notes you'd expect to find in a perfectly pulled shot.

5. The milk

The success of your coffee now rests on nailing the creamy, velvety milk. Take a stainless steel pitcher, wider at the bottom than at the top, and half-fill it with cold, fresh whole milk.

Blast the steam wand into a dishtowel to purge any water built up in the pipes, then insert the wand into the milk. Turn on the steam and bring the nozzle to the surface until you hear air being sucked into the milk. It should make a gentle *phsh*, *phsh* sound, not a loud sucking noise. Do this for just a few seconds, then submerge the wand and tilt the pitcher slightly to create a whirlpool effect that produces micro-foam—milk like silk. It's important not to suck too much air into the milk in those first few seconds, as it will create big bubbles that are difficult to get rid of.

When your hand can no longer stand the heat from the bottom of the pitcher, the milk is hot enough and ready to pour. Tap the pitcher on the countertop to help knock out any large bubbles that have snuck in, then "back-blend" (swirl) the milk to keep it silky and smooth.

6. The pour

With your pitcher held high, start pouring the milk, dropping closer to the cup to create latte art patterns on top of the finished drink.

Relax and enjoy!

Coffee types

Coffee was always going to be one of the cornerstones of Ginger & White. And while the London coffee scene has come of age in recent times, with many different brewing methods on offer, we have chosen to concentrate on the union of humble espresso and milk like silk. Ever true to our motto "We *don't* do Grande!" we're proud to think that, over the years, we've helped steer Londoners toward smaller, stronger, and, ultimately, tastier coffee.

ESPRESSO—about 1 fl. oz. extracted in 27–30 seconds, this is where the perfect coffee begins; concentrating all the aromas and flavors of the bean into a smooth, golden liquid.

MACCHIATO—an espresso shot just "stained" with hot milk to take the edge off.

CORTADO—a single espresso combined with an equal amount of creamy milk; it's a smaller version of a flat white.

LONG BLACK—a double espresso with a dash more water.

CAPPUCCINO—a double espresso topped with plenty of velvety micro-foam; this is the strongest of the milky coffees, traditionally drunk at breakfast.

FLAT WHITE—a double espresso combined with an equal amount of creamy milk, somewhere between a cappuccino and a caffe latte; antipodean in origin.

CAFFE LATTE—a single espresso with creamy milk in an 8-oz. glass; the milkiest coffee of them all.

Banana & wheat germ smoothie

The perfect bananas for this recipe should be yellow with just a few brown spots. Slice and freeze them before use so that the smoothie is beautifully chilled with no need to add ice. This will keep it thick and luscious.

Place all the ingredients in a blender and blitz for 30–45 seconds, until smooth. Serve immediately.

SERVES 1

6 pieces of frozen banana (about 4 oz.)

¼ cup plain yogurt

½ cup milk

1 tsp honey

1 scant tsp wheat germ

Grapefruit & orange morning juice

Mixing a dash of freshly squeezed, mouth-puckering grapefruit into your morning O.J. gives it a really tangy edge. It feels more cleansing and better for you than just sweet orange juice and is packed full of vitamin C. Look out for navel oranges, which yield lots more juice than regular ones.

Squeeze the juice out of the grapefruit and the oranges. Pour into a glass filled with ice and serve immediately.

SERVES 1

1 grapefruit, halved

3 oranges, halved

ice

Bloody Mary

It's very easy to throw together an average Bloody Mary, but for a drink that makes your taste buds tingle, every ingredient needs to earn its place. We found our sweet spot with a clean, crisp vodka from Suffolk, which we layer with just the right amount of tomato juice spiked with the classic condiments. Be warned: it is seriously spicy.

Sprinkle some celery salt onto a saucer. Run the lemon wedge around the rim of a glass, then dip the rim in the celery salt.

Fill the glass with ice and add the vodka. Squeeze the lemon into it, then add the wedge to the glass. Add the tomato juice, plus a dash of Tabasco and Worcestershire sauce, then stir and taste. Adjust the spice level by adding more sauce as necessary.

Garnish the drink with the cucumber or celery stalk, then add a twist of black pepper on top.

SERVES 1

celery salt

lemon wedge

ice

2 fl. oz. clean, crisp vodka

½ cup tomato juice

Tabasco sauce

Worcestershire sauce

cucumber slice or celery stalk, to garnish

freshly ground black pepper

Blood orange mimosa

We're bordering on obsessed with the darkly crimson blood orange. It adds a splash of vivid color to a wintry brunch table, and its juice is an excellent addition to a lunchtime glass of champagne.

Juice the blood oranges into a pitcher.

Pour the juice into 8–10 champagne flutes, depending on size, until they are about one third full. Top up with the champagne.

SERVES 8–10

10 blood oranges, halved

bottle of chilled champagne

Hot chocolate
with marshmallows

We use luxurious organic, plain chocolate, which, when mixed with creamy milk, is pretty much the eighth wonder of the world. Just ask Wendy, our resident hot chocolate connoisseur, who you'll find in our Hampstead branch on any given day. To spice things up a little, try using chocolate flavored with mint, chili, or bitter orange.

Put the chocolate and cocoa into an enamel mug. Add the water and stir to make a paste.

Steam the milk, stretching it with your steam wand, or heat it on the stove to just below boiling point. Whisk it into the chocolate paste, then float the marshmallows on top and serve immediately.

SERVES 1

2 heaping tbsp grated dark chocolate (at least 70 percent cocoa solids)

1 heaping tbsp cocoa powder

1 tbsp boiling water

1 cup whole milk

2 big marshmallows or a handful of mini ones

Toasted banana bread
with vanilla cream cheese, rhubarb, & raspberries

Here's another weekend favorite—one of the prettiest brunch dishes. When young, Barbie-pink rhubarb is in season, we roast it in the oven with just a shake of sugar so that it keeps its color and shape. The sharpness of this topping goes perfectly with the warm and spicy banana bread, which is another of our guilty pleasures.

Preheat the oven to 360°F. Grease a 2-lb. bread pan and baseline it with nonstick parchment paper.

Cream the butter and sugar in a bowl until pale and fluffy. Beat in about a quarter of the eggs at a time.

In another bowl, mash the bananas with a fork and stir in the vanilla extract. Mix into the creamed butter, then fold in all the remaining dry ingredients. Finally, stir in the buttermilk until you have a smooth batter.

Pour the mixture into the prepared pan, using a flexible spatula to get it all out of the bowl, and bake on the middle shelf for 30–40 minutes, until a skewer inserted into the center comes out clean. Remove the bread from the oven and allow to cool in the pan, but leave the oven on.

Now prepare the rhubarb. Put the vanilla sugar into a baking sheet, toss the rhubarb in it, and bake for 15 minutes, until just tender. Allow to cool.

Preheat the broiler on a medium setting.

Meanwhile, make the vanilla cream cheese by beating the cream cheese, yogurt, and vanilla bean paste together until smooth. Sift in the powdered sugar and beat again.

Toast 4 thick slices of the banana bread under the broiler on both sides. Watch them carefully because they can quickly blacken around the edges.

To serve, top each slice with a scoop of vanilla cream cheese, 3–4 rhubarb pieces, and a scattering of raspberries. Finish with a drizzle of honey and serve.

SERVES 4

1 stick unsalted butter, softened, plus extra for greasing

1⅔ cups unrefined superfine sugar

2 free-range eggs, beaten

3 very ripe bananas

¼ tsp vanilla extract

2 cups all-purpose flour

1 tsp baking soda

½ tsp fine salt

½ tsp ground cinnamon

generous pinch of ground allspice

½ cup buttermilk

1 punnet raspberries

3½ tbsp clear honey

For the rhubarb

2 tbsp vanilla sugar

11 oz. pink forced rhubarb, cut into 3-in. pieces

For the vanilla cream cheese

¾ cup cream cheese

⅓ cup plain yogurt

⅛ tsp vanilla bean paste

2 tbsp powdered sugar

Spiced plum & almond French toast

For this recipe, we soak slices of day-old bloomer in plenty of cream, eggs, and milk and fry them until crisp and golden. We then pile them high with roasted British plums, which reach their best at the tail end of the summer. Be sure not to overcook them or they'll turn mushy and lose their shape. In the early summer, we use berries rather than plums; and once the plum season has passed, we use bananas.

Preheat the oven to 390°F.

Place the plums in a baking sheet and sprinkle with the light brown sugar, spices, and water. Cover with foil and roast for 25 minutes, until the fruit is soft but still holding its shape. Leave the oven on.

Meanwhile, put the eggs, cream, milk, vanilla paste, and granulated sugar into a bowl and beat them together. Add the bread, turn to coat thoroughly, and allow to soak for 30 minutes.

When the plums are ready, set them aside at room temperature for the syrup to thicken or drain the syrup into a saucepan and reduce it over a medium heat until it has thickened.

Heat the sunflower oil in a skillet and fry the soaked bread on each side until crisp (you may need to do this in batches). Transfer the bread to a cookie sheet and place in the hot oven for 2–3 minutes, until puffed up.

Cut the bread in half diagonally and place on 2 plates. Top each piece with with the roasted plum halves and drizzle the syrup all over. Sprinkle with sliced almonds, if desired, and serve immediately.

SERVES 2

4 red plums, halved and pitted
5 tsp light brown sugar
pinch of ground cinnamon
1 star anise
1 tbsp water
2 free-range eggs
1 tbsp heavy cream
2 tbsp whole milk
smear of vanilla paste
3½ tbsp granulated sugar
2 thick, crustless slices of white farmhouse bread, preferably 1 day old
3⅔ tbsp sunflower oil
⅛ cup toasted sliced almonds, to garnish (optional)

Nutty honey granola
with berry & spice compote

Similar to muesli, granola is easy to make and keeps for a month. The trick is getting it to bake to a crisp texture without creating any bitter flavors, which is what happens if you overdo it. Texture and color are not good checks for readiness because the mixture will feel soft until it completely cools. Our mug test will help you judge it accurately.

Preheat the oven to 320°F.

Place the honey, sugar, oil, and cinnamon in a small saucepan over a low heat and warm, without stirring, until the sugar has dissolved.

Put the oats, nuts, seeds, and salt into a large bowl. Pour in the hot, sugary mixture and stir well.

Tip the granola into 2 large roasting pans, making a layer no more than 1 in. deep. Bake for 25–35 minutes, then stir to swap the position of the darker oats at the edges with the lighter oats in the middle. Bake for another 20–30 minutes, until pale golden. To check that it is done, put a spoonful of the granola into a mug and rattle it around until it is completely cool. If it makes a clattery sound against the cup, it is crunchy enough. If not, bake for a little longer.

Allow the mixture to cool for 10 minutes before stirring in the cranberries, raisins, or dried fruit, then set aside to cool completely. Store in an airtight container for up to 1 month.

We serve the granola with thick yogurt drizzled with honey, a spoonful of our berry and spice compote, and a spoonful of berries, if they are in season.

MAKES 2 LB.

¾ cup clear honey

⅔ cup superfine sugar

4½ tbsp sunflower oil

1 tsp ground cinnamon

2½ cups jumbo oats

3¼ tbsp sliced almonds

½ cup walnuts, roughly chopped

⅔ cup sunflower seeds

⅓ cup pumpkin seeds

⅔ cup sesame seeds

½ tsp table salt

¾ cup dried cranberries, golden raisins, dried bananas, or any chopped dried fruit

To serve

thick plain or Greek yogurt

clear honey

Berry & Spice Compote (*see* page 157)

fresh berries (optional)

Fruity crumble muffins

Every morning, our shops are filled with the sweet scent of buttery crumble muffins. Baking these is the first job of the day so that we can have them ready for our first customers on their way to work. Originally, we studded them with seasonal fruit, but our chefs have since come up with so many flavors that we could probably dedicate an entire book to them. The nutty crumble topping gives them a great British twist. To highlight the changes, try replacing the fruit according to the variations opposite.

Preheat the oven to 360°F. Line a 6-hole muffin pan with paper bake cups, or set out a silicone muffin pan.

Put the butter into a glass pitcher and heat in the microwave until melted. Add the buttermilk, then whisk in the egg.

Combine all the dry ingredients (except the fruit) in a bowl and add the egg mixture, stirring until there are no floury pockets (it can be a little bit lumpy). Fold in the fruit, then spoon the mixture into the paper cases or silicone muffin tray, almost to the top of each hole.

To make the crumble topping, place the flour and butter in a bowl and blend until the mixture resembles coarse, clumpy bread crumbs. Stir in the sugar and nuts.

Pile a heaping 2 tablespoons of the crumble mixture onto each muffin and bake for 25–30 minutes. Turn out of the pan and place upside down to cool (the muffins are top-heavy, so doing this prevents the lighter cake underneath from getting squashed).

MAKES 6

½ stick unsalted butter

⅔ cup buttermilk

1 free-range egg

1⅔ cups all-purpose flour

1 tsp baking powder

¼ tsp baking soda

⅓ cup superfine sugar

pinch of salt

⅔ cup chopped fresh fruit

For the crumble topping

½ cup all-purpose flour

3 tbsp chilled butter, cubed

1½ tbsp granulated sugar

½ cup almonds, walnuts, or pine nuts, chopped

VARIATIONS

Rhubarb, vanilla, & almond muffins:
Thinly slice 2 stalks of tender forced rhubarb and add to the muffin batter along with ¼ tsp vanilla paste. Use sliced almonds in the crumble topping instead of chopped. Bake as opposite.

Apple, cinnamon, & walnut muffins:
Peel and core 2 Granny Smith apples, then coarsely grate them into the muffin batter. Add 1 tsp cinnamon to the crumble topping and choose chopped walnuts. Bake as opposite.

Chocolate swirl muffins:
Mix ½ cup cocoa powder with 1 tbsp boiling water until smooth, then lightly swirl into the muffin batter to create a marbled effect. Stir in ⅓ cup white chocolate chips and grate some dark chocolate on top instead of using the crumble topping. Bake as opposite.

Mixed berry muffins:
Add ½ cup raspberries and/or blueberries to the batter. Omit the crumble and scatter a few more berries on top so that they burst during baking and give a sneak preview of what's inside.

Roasted peanut butter

Our peanut butter is legendary in certain parts of northwest London. Such is its popularity that we're a little scared to part with this recipe in case our customers desert us. It is crazily simple: you just need to be brave enough to roast the nuts to a good golden color and have a flair for balancing sweet with salt. Unlike jam, peanut butter is not boiled, so it must always be kept refrigerated and eaten within 6 weeks.

Preheat the oven to 360°F. Sterilize your jars and lids (*see* tip, below).

Place the peanuts in a large roasting pan and roast until golden (35–45 minutes), stirring if they start to brown unevenly. The skins will peel open to reveal a developing tan underneath. When the peanuts are deeply bronzed, as though just back from the Caribbean, they are ready.

Transfer the nuts, still in their skins, to a blender or food processor. Add the remaining ingredients and blitz until combined.

Scrape down the sides of the blender or bowl with a spatula and blend again. You need a textured but spreadable paste, so add more oil if it feels too stiff. Taste and add more salt or sugar as you prefer. Using a spatula, transfer the mixture to your sterilized jars. Seal tightly, then label and date.

MAKES 1 LB. 9 OZ.

1 lb. unsalted peanuts, with skin

1 tsp sea salt

¾ cup peanut oil

1 tbsp clear honey

1 tbsp demerara sugar

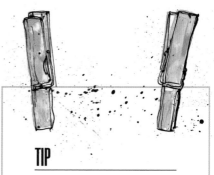

TIP

It's important to wash and sterilize both jars and lids before storing preserves in them so that they are free of bacteria that could taint the content. We wash ours in the dishwasher, then place them upside down in a low oven for 30 minutes to ensure that they are thoroughly dry.

Spicy baked beans
with red bell peppers, chorizo, & feta cheese

Our famous baked beans have been on the menu since the day we first opened our doors in Hampstead, and they epitomize our playful approach to food. Beans have always been a guilty pleasure of ours, so we gave them an adult twist, balancing the sweetness with a sour tang and spiking them with chili. In their latest makeover, we top them with fried slices of chorizo and salty feta cheese, so we're more in love with them now than ever. They're always the first thing that Tonia and Emma order when they're in the café.

Drain the beans, transfer them to a saucepan, and cover with plenty of water (do not add salt). Bring to a boil, then cover, reduce the heat, and simmer for 45 minutes, until tender. Drain again.

Meanwhile, heat the butter in a large, flameproof casserole dish and fry the onions and peppers until the onion is very soft and sweet, but not colored. Cover the dish and cook over a low heat for 30 minutes, stirring occasionally.

When the onion mixture is soft and sticky, add the mustard powder, paprika, pepper flakes, molasses or sugar, tomatoes, boiling water, and vinegar. Add the beans, cover with a lid, and simmer over a low heat for 1 hour. Season with the salt, stir well, and taste. If too sweet, add more salt and 2–3 tablespoons more vinegar. If too dry, add a little more boiling water. If too runny, cook uncovered until the sauce has thickened a little; it will thicken more on cooling.

To make the topping, place the chorizo in a heavy-based pan and fry until crisp.

Reheat the beans and serve them in a bowl topped with the fried chorizo, crumbled feta cheese, and a sprinkling of parsley. Serve with buttered toast on the side.

SERVES 4

2 cups dried mixed beans, such as navy beans, lima beans, and chickpeas, soaked overnight in 3 times their depth of water

½ stick butter

2 red onions, thickly sliced

2 red bell peppers, seeded and thickly sliced

1 tsp English mustard powder

1 tsp smoked sweet paprika

½ tsp red pepper flakes

⅓ cup molasses or brown sugar

14 oz. can plum tomatoes

2 cups boiling water

4 tbsp cider vinegar

2 tsp salt

buttered sourdough or granary toast, to serve

For the topping

7 oz. chunky chorizo, sliced

⅓ cup crumbled feta cheese

2 sprigs flat-leaf parsley, leaves picked and roughly chopped

Corn fritters
with chili jam & slow-roasted tomatoes

Although this is a typically Australian brunch dish, we felt that it deserved a place on our menu because we all adore it. We sell a lot of these fritters on weekends, often with our amazing bacon, and, when avocados are nutty and creamy, we mash them up with lime juice and use them in place of the crème fraîche.

Place the flour, baking soda, semolina, and cayenne pepper in a mixing bowl.

In a separate bowl, whisk together the eggs and yogurt. Mix in the corn and scallions, then pour the mixture into the flour and stir until combined. Season well with salt and pepper. The batter should have a fairly firm consistency.

Heat 1 tablespoon of oil in a skillet over a low–medium heat, then drop 3 tablespoons of the batter into the pan to create 3 small fritters. Cook for 4–6 minutes, turning halfway through, until thoroughly cooked and golden on both sides. Repeat with the remaining batter, keeping the cooked fritters warm.

Serve each person 3 fritters with 2 slow-roasted tomato halves, 2 slices of bacon, a scoop of crème fraîche or sour cream, and a blob of chili jam. Garnish with arugula leaves.

SERVES 4

½ cup self-rising flour

½ tsp baking soda

⅓ cup semolina

pinch of cayenne pepper

2 free-range eggs

¾ cup Greek yogurt

14 oz. (drained weight) canned or frozen corn, defrosted if frozen

6 scallions, trimmed and sliced

½ tsp salt

freshly ground black pepper

sunflower oil, for frying

To serve

8 halves of Slow-roasted Tomatoes (*see* page 148)

8 slices of Canadian bacon, fried

½ cup crème fraîche or sour cream

4 tbsp chili jam

arugula leaves

Four types of mini frittatas

EACH RECIPE MAKES 4–6

Adding cream to the eggs in these recipes gives the frittatas a smoother texture and stabilizes them. It's also totally delicious and just a tiny bit indulgent. We like to bake them in 4-hole Yorkshire pudding trays, but you can use muffin pans instead—being deeper, they might take about 5 minutes longer to bake. Serve with a sharply dressed salad for a light lunch.

Cheddar, thyme, & caramelized onion

Preheat the oven to 390°F. Drizzle 1 teaspoon olive oil into the holes in your baking pan(s).

Place the butter, onions, and thyme in a small saucepan. Cover and cook over a very low heat for 15 minutes, until the onion is caramelized. Add the garlic and cook for another 2 minutes.

Meanwhile, put the eggs, yolks, cream, and cheese into a bowl and beat together. Add the onion mixture, then spoon into the prepared baking pan(s). Place on a cookie sheet and bake for 25–30 minutes, until golden and not too wobbly in the middle. Cool in the pan, then serve.

olive oil, for greasing
1 tbsp butter
2 white onions, sliced
few sprigs of thyme
2 garlic cloves, chopped
6 free-range eggs, plus 2 yolks
2½ cups heavy cream
1 cup grated sharp cheddar cheese

Chorizo & bell pepper

Preheat the oven to 390°F. Drizzle 1 teaspoon olive oil into the holes in your baking pan(s).

Put the eggs, yolk, and cream into a bowl, add salt and pepper, and beat together. Add the thyme, peppers, and half the chorizo. Divide between the prepared holes in the baking pan(s). Top with the remaining chorizo and season with salt and pepper.

Place on a cookie sheet and bake for 25–30 minutes, until golden around the edges and not too wobbly in the middle. Cool in the pan, then serve.

olive oil, for greasing
6 free-range eggs, plus 1 yolk
2 cups heavy cream
few sprigs of thyme
3½ oz. roasted red bell peppers in oil, drained and sliced
7 oz. chorizo, sliced
salt and pepper

Feta cheese, tomato, & spinach

Preheat the oven to 390°F. Drizzle 1 teaspoon olive oil into the holes in your baking pan(s).

Place the spinach in a large saucepan with 1 tablespoon olive oil, cover, and heat until wilted. Drain and chop.

Put the eggs, yolk, and cream into a bowl, add salt and pepper, and beat together.

Combine the spinach with the egg mixture and half the feta cheese. Divide between the prepared holes in the baking pan(s). Top with the remaining feta cheese and the slow-roasted tomatoes, drizzle with oil, and season with salt and pepper. Place on a cookie sheet and bake for 25–30 minutes, until golden around the edges and not too wobbly in the middle. Cool in the pan, then serve.

1 tbsp olive oil, plus extra for greasing

14 oz. baby spinach

5 free-range eggs, plus 1 yolk

2 cups heavy cream

1 ⅓ cups cubed or crumbled feta cheese

6 halves of Slow-roasted Tomatoes (*see* page 148)

salt and pepper

Salmon, onion, & anchovy

Preheat the oven to 390°F. Drizzle 1 teaspoon olive oil into the holes in your baking pan(s).

Put the eggs, yolks, cream, and herbs into a bowl and beat together.

Divide the salmon, scallions, and anchovies between the prepared holes in the baking pan(s). Top up with the egg and cream mixture and place on a cookie sheet. Bake for 25–30 minutes, until golden around the edges and not too wobbly in the middle. Cool in the pan, then serve.

olive oil, for greasing

6 free-range eggs, plus 2 yolks

2½ cups heavy cream

3 tbsp chopped herbs, such as dill, parsley, and/or chives

5½ oz. salmon fillet or smoked salmon, chopped

6 scallions, sliced

6 anchovy fillets, chopped

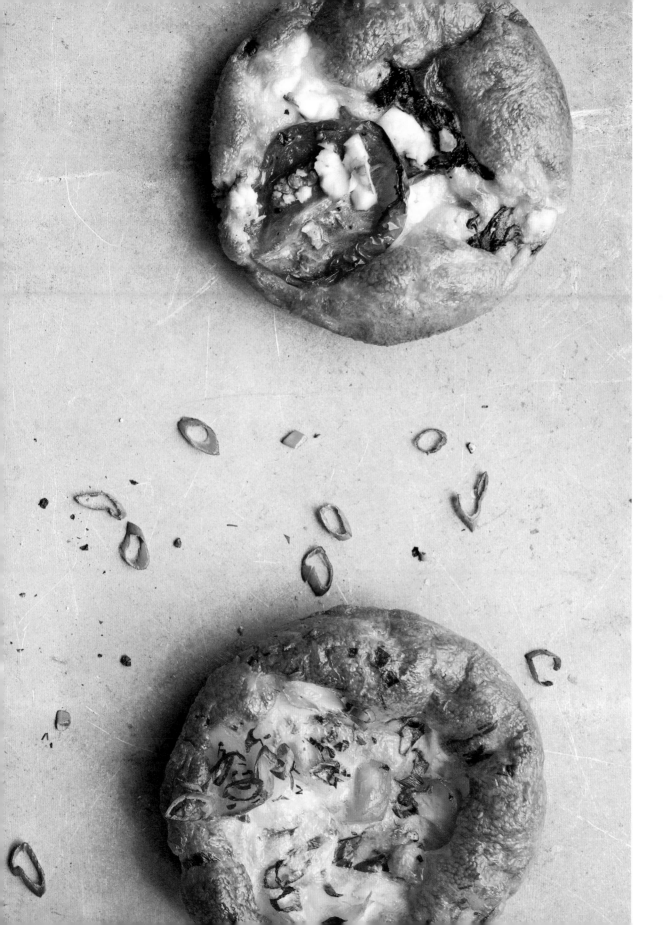

Fried duck eggs
with blood sausage & sourdough croutons

We love the pear, date, and ale chutney that one of our suppliers makes for us, but you can use any fruity relish to accompany this dish or replace it with any of your favorite condiments. We use the fairytale white eggs that ducks lay in the daylight hours of spring and summer; they tend to be larger than hens' eggs, so need a little bit longer when frying.

Warm 4 plates. Heat 1 tablespoon of the olive oil in a large skillet and fry the blood sausage over a medium heat until crisp.

Add the croutons and heat for a few minutes to warm through and combine with the other flavors. Tip into a bowl, cover with foil, and keep warm.

Wipe out the pan, add 2 tablespoons of the olive oil, and place over a high heat. When hot, crack 4 of the eggs into the pan, cover with a lid, and cook for 1–2 minutes, until the whites are set but the yolks are molten. Transfer to 2 warm plates and keep warm. Cook the remaining eggs in the same way and put them on the remaining warm plates.

Dust all the eggs with the red pepper flakes, scatter the crouton and blood sausage mixture over them, then add a spoonful of the relish onto each plate. Garnish with parsley and serve immediately.

SERVES 4

5 tbsp olive oil
11 oz. blood sausage, roughly chopped
3½ oz. Rosemary Sourdough Croutons (*see* page 155)
8 free-range eggs
¼ tsp red pepper flakes
6 tbsp fruity relish
4 tbsp roughly chopped flat-leaf parsley leaves, to garnish

Soft-boiled eggs
with toast "soldiers"

The very precise way in which we cook our boiled eggs sums up our attitude to food: they have to be perfect every time. Tonia's mom, who used to keep chickens, came up with this great way of cooking perfect boiled eggs. Instead of doing them at a rolling boil, which can make them tough, she rests them in hot water, which coaxes them into a creamy set white with a molten golden yolk. Topped with little woolly hats to keep them warm, what could be better? Plus, for added fun, we slice our toast in the traditionally British style of "soldiers" to dunk into the eggs!

Bring a medium saucepan of water to a boil. Turn the heat down to the gentlest simmer and lower the eggs into the water using a slotted spoon. Boil for 1 minute, then take off the heat, cover with a lid, and set aside for 4 minutes (use a timer for this).

Toast the bread, then butter it and slice it into soldiers less than 1 in. thick.

Put 4 eggcups on 2 small plates with a teaspoon and the toast soldiers. When the timer goes off, make sure you're ready to sit down, as the eggs need to be cracked and eaten immediately. Enjoy!

SERVES 2

4 free-range eggs, at room temperature

4 thick slices of white bread, from a farmhouse loaf

salted butter, softened

Chorizo & slow-roasted tomato omelet

This is one of the simplest and tastiest recipes in the book. As unashamed toast addicts, we serve a lot of our breakfast dishes on toast, but this one is completely gluten-free. A scattering of Rosemary Sourdough Croutons (*see* page 155) or a drizzle of garlicky yogurt can elevate the humble omelet into something sublime.

Place a dry, heavy-based skillet over a high heat. When hot, cook the chorizo for 1 minute on each side until crisp. Transfer to a plate.

Add the olive oil to the hot pan, then pour in the beaten eggs. Season and cook, tilting the pan so that the omelet sets in a thin layer, almost like a pancake.

Add the slow-roasted tomatoes and reserved chorizo and cook until just set on top. Sprinkle with the parsley.

Using a large spatula or palette knife, lift or slide the open omelet onto a plate and serve immediately.

SERVES 1

2 oz. chorizo, thinly sliced

1 tbsp olive oil

2 free-range eggs, beaten

salt and pepper

5 halves of Slow-roasted Tomatoes (*see* page 148)

handful of flat-leaf parsley, leaves picked

Scrambled eggs
with buttermilk & smoked salmon

Our secret is out: we add buttermilk to scrambled eggs. This gives them a lighter texture than when adding cream, but a slightly different (almost cheesy) texture than when adding milk. It's important not to have the heat too high, or the eggs can quickly overcook. Also, take them off the heat while they are still a little runny on top and they will finish cooking in the warmth of the pan. Another trick is to have your toast ready and waiting so you can take the eggs out of the pan the moment they are cooked to perfection. Egg cookery is all about precision, and being a pedant really helps!

Crack the eggs into a bowl, add the buttermilk and seasoning, then whisk until just blended—don't overbeat them.

Toast the bread, get your plates and silverware ready, and have some softened butter to hand.

Heat a skillet over a medium heat and melt the butter. Turn down the heat as low as possible, then pour in the eggs and let them almost set underneath. Using a spatula, fold them into the center—don't break them up too vigorously or you'll get a weird broken-up texture. When the eggs are still runny on top, remove them from the heat and continue to fold them so that they are only just cooked through.

Quickly butter your toast and pile the eggs on it. Fold the salmon over the eggs and finish with chopped chives, then add a twist of black pepper on top.

SERVES 2

6 free-range eggs

½ cup buttermilk

salt and pepper

4 slices of sourdough bread

1 ½ tbsp butter, plus extra for spreading

5 oz. smoked salmon

chopped chives, to garnish

Chorizo, avocado, & lime on toast

There are few dishes that are not improved by the intense, smoky flavor of chorizo. We slice and fry it lightly until it is crisp and the paprika-stained juices are released. When avocados are at their peak, their flesh should be creamy with a slightly nutty edge, but in our opinion they need to be perked up a bit with a shake of Tabasco, a squeeze of lime, and a tickle of salt just to tease out their flavor.

Put the avocado flesh into a bowl, add the lime juice, and roughly mash together. Add a shake of Tabasco, a good twist of black pepper, and the salt. Cover with plastic wrap to prevent the flesh from turning brown.

Place a dry, heavy-based skillet over a high heat. When hot, briefly fry the chorizo on both sides until it releases its fat.

Heat a griddle pan until very hot. Add the ciabatta and toast on both sides.

Spread the avocado mixture on the toast, top with a few slices of warm chorizo, some slow-roasted tomatoes, arugula leaves, and a drizzle of olive oil.

SERVES 4

2 ripe avocados, halved and pitted

juice of ½ lime

Tabasco sauce

freshly ground black pepper

½ tsp sea salt

7 oz. chorizo, thinly sliced in extreme diagonals (almost horizontal)

1 ciabatta loaf, cut in half horizontally and then into 4 widthwise

12 halves of Slow-roasted Tomatoes (*see* page 148)

handful of arugula leaves

extra virgin olive oil, for drizzling

Portobello mushrooms
with roasted garlic mayo on potato sourdough

Roasting mushrooms really brings out their earthy flavor, providing a satisfying alternative to meat for vegetarians. We serve them on a thick-crust, chewy sourdough made with potatoes, which provides a good contrast to their soft texture. If you don't have time to make the Roasted Garlic Mayonnaise, simply crush a quarter of a garlic clove and stir it into some mayo or, even easier, rub the toast with a cut garlic clove instead.

Preheat the oven to 390°F.

Clean the mushrooms, discarding the stalks. Place them in a sheet pan, drizzle with the olive oil, and season with salt and pepper.

Roast the mushrooms for 15 minutes, until softened. Turn them over and roast for an additional 10 minutes.

Toast the sourdough on both sides, then spread the garlic mayo on the toast and divide it between 2 plates. Top each slice with a mushroom.

Dress the arugula in olive oil with a little salt and pepper. Pile on top of the mushrooms and serve.

SERVES 2

4 portobello mushrooms

1 tbsp extra virgin olive oil, plus extra for dressing

salt and pepper

4 thick slices of potato sourdough

4 tbsp Roasted Garlic Mayonnaise (*see* page 150)

handful of arugula leaves

Kedgeree

On weekends, we serve tradional British–Indian kedgeree for breakfast, but we also serve it for dinner because we just adore it. A good kedgeree has all of the components cooked to perfection and lightly combined so they don't break up too much. Ours is a buttery dish with fluffy grains of lightly spiced rice and plump pieces of smoky fish, finished off with eggs that are just runny in the center.

Melt 3½ tbsp of the butter in a saucepan over a low heat. Add the onions, cover with a lid, and cook for 10 minutes, until soft and translucent.

Meanwhile, simmer the eggs for 4 minutes, but allow them to sit in the hot water for 6 minutes. Drain, then run cold water over them until cool. Peel and halve, then set aside.

Place the rice in a saucepan with the water, bay leaves, and salt. Bring to a boil, clamp on a lid, and simmer on the lowest possible heat for 5 minutes. Set aside, keeping the lid on. By the time you're ready to use it, the water will have been absorbed and the grains will be fluffy.

Add the spices to the onion and cook for 2 minutes, until they are golden brown.

Place the smoked haddock in a pan, skin-side down, and pour in the milk. Simmer very gently for 3–4 minutes, until the thickest part has lost its transparency. Drain, remove the skin and bones, and flake into large chunks.

Heat the remaining butter in a large skillet and add the cooked rice and spiced onions. Fold in the flaked haddock, being careful not to break it up too much. Top with the halved boiled eggs. (The kedgeree can be served straight from the pan or arranged on individual plates.)

Serve with the lemon wedges, a scattering of cilantro leaves, and a good twist of black pepper. Offer mango chutney and plain yogurt in separate bowls for people to help themselves.

SERVES 4

1 stick butter

2 large white onions, thinly sliced

4 free-range eggs

1 cup Basmati rice, washed several times until the water is clear

1 cup cold water

2 bay leaves

½ tsp salt

1 tbsp mild curry powder

5 cardamom pods, crushed

1 lb. 5 oz. undyed smoked haddock

1¼ cups milk

To serve

2 lemons, cut into wedges

cilantro leaves

freshly ground black pepper

mango chutney

plain yogurt

Lunch

Smoked mackerel, fennel, & chickpea salad
with horseradish & yogurt dressing

Here's a summery salad that could be served as a great appetizer, too. Come wintertime, we warm it up by roasting the fennel until it's slightly frazzled and add some Slow-roasted Tomatoes (*see* page 148), too. The chickpeas can be swapped for any legume you like, or even some couscous dressed in lemon and olive oil. Similarly, use any other lettuce leaves in place of the baby gem.

To make the yogurt and horseradish dressing, whisk all the ingredients together in a bowl.

Flake the mackerel into bite-size pieces. Cut each lettuce half into 4 wedges.

Put the chickpeas into a bowl and mix with half the olive oil, plus some salt and pepper.

Finely slice the fennel and place it in a bowl with the tomatoes and scallions. Add the remaining olive oil, the lemon juice, and extra salt and pepper and toss well.

Layer the lettuce and chickpeas in a shallow serving bowl with the dressed fennel, tomatoes, and scallions. Scatter the smoked mackerel on top and drizzle the 4 salads with half the dressing, serving the extra on the side.

SERVES 4

11 oz. smoked mackerel fillet, skinned and boned

4 baby gem lettuces, halved

14 oz. canned chickpeas, rinsed and drained

4 tbsp olive oil

salt and pepper

1 fennel bulb, trimmed

⅔ cup cherry tomatoes, halved

bunch of scallions, sliced

juice of ½ lemon

For the yogurt & horseradish dressing

¾ cup plain yogurt

2⅔ cups extra virgin olive oil

2 tbsp lemon juice

2 tsp hot horseradish sauce

Roasted garlic & lemon thyme chicken
with tomato & sourdough salad

Chicken thighs have much more flavor than breast meat, and cooking them slowly gives them a lovely soft texture, so the meat just falls apart. We have served this dish at several summer parties because it always goes down amazingly well. The chicken is accompanied by our version of the Tuscan salad panzanella, and we always warn our guests that it is the garlic lovers' option.

Roughly chop the tomatoes and bread into 1-in. cubes. Combine in a bowl. Whisk together the olive oil, vinegar, garlic, and capers, season well with salt and pepper, then pour over the bread mixture. Stir well, then set aside for 3–4 hours so that the flavors meld together.

Preheat the oven to 320°F.

Now prepare the chicken. Combine the olive oil, garlic cloves, lemon wedges, and lemon thyme in a roasting pan. Season with salt and pepper, then add the chicken and toss well to coat. Pour in the wine, cover tightly with foil, and cook for 2 hours. Remove the foil and cook for an additional 45 minutes, until the chicken skin is crisp.

Just before serving, toss the salad and sprinkle with the baby basil leaves. Put 2 chicken thighs on each plate, add a drizzle of the cooking juices (discard the lemons), and serve with the salad.

SERVES 6

1 lb. 9 oz. plum tomatoes

11 oz. sourdough bread, left out overnight

4 tbsp extra virgin olive oil

2 tbsp red wine vinegar

1 garlic clove, crushed

1 tbsp small capers, drained

salt and pepper

handful of baby basil leaves

For the chicken

4 tbsp extra virgin olive oil

6 garlic cloves, unpeeled

2 unwaxed lemons, each cut into 8 wedges

2–3 sprigs lemon thyme

12 chicken thighs, with skin on

7–10 fl. oz. white wine

Endive & radicchio salad
with roasted parsnips, blue cheese, & grapes

There is nothing quite like roasted parsnips, especially when you bring chili and honey into the equation. This was a salad born out of the leftovers of a Sunday roast dinner and is one of the loveliest winter salads we serve. Our preferred cheese for this is a creamy blue. If you find blue cheese too tangy, you can substitute in feta cheese.

Preheat the oven to 390°F.

Place the parsnips in a roasting pan. Mix together the red pepper flakes, cinnamon, and oil and drizzle over the parsnips. Roast for 25–30 minutes. When the parsnips are soft and cooked through, drizzle with the honey and roast for an additional 15 minutes, until sticky, golden, and crisp.

Transfer the parsnips to a bowl. Add the grapes, cheese, and half the dressing. Toss well.

Divide the endive and radicchio between 4 serving plates and top with the parsnip mixture, finishing with a scattering of walnuts. Serve with the remaining dressing on the side.

SERVES 4

2 lb. 4 oz. parsnips, peeled and quartered lengthwise

1 tsp red pepper flakes

1 tsp ground cinnamon

6 tbsp olive oil

1 tbsp clear honey

small bunch of seedless red grapes, halved

1 1/3 cups crumbled or cubed blue cheese

1/2 cup Canola Oil & English Mustard Dressing (*see* page 151)

6 heads of Belgian endive, leaves separated and cut in half lengthwise

1/2 head of radicchio, shredded

1/2 cup walnuts, roughly chopped

Corned beef, red onion, & potato salad
with anchovies & capers

We introduced meltingly tender corned beef to our menu when we opened our café in Hampstead. We slowly braise our own corned beef for hours until tender, then shred it for this wintry weekend lunch salad. The capers and anchovies add piquancy, but it's the salt beef that takes the limelight.

Preheat the oven to 390°F.

Put the potatoes and onions into a roasting pan. Add the oil and anchovy fillets and toss well. Roast for 30–40 minutes, until golden and soft.

Place the corned beef in a large bowl and add the potatoes, onions, and parsley.

Mix the mustard powder and honey into the dressing, add the capers, then pour over the beef mixture and toss well. Taste and add salt if you wish.

SERVES 4

2 lb. 4 oz. new potatoes, halved

3 red onions, each cut into 8 wedges

4 tbsp extra virgin olive oil

6 salted anchovy fillets, rinsed and chopped

1 lb. 2 oz. Braised Corned Beef (*see* page 153), chopped or shredded

large bunch of flat-leaf parsley, leaves picked

1 tbsp English mustard powder

1 tbsp honey

1 cup Canola Oil & English Mustard Dressing (*see* page 151)

2 tbsp capers, drained

salt (optional)

Smoked ham, lima bean, & gherkin salad
with slow-roasted tomatoes

We're huge fans of ham hock, so shredded slow-braised ham hock would naturally be our choice for this salad. Failing that, you can buy a chunk of ham and shred it yourself. When we want a change, we have been known to make this salad using tuna in olive oil, which is incredibly delicious as well.

Put the lima beans into a bowl and add the gherkins or cornichons, onion, parsley, and dressing. Toss well.

Divide the salad between 4 plates, top with the ham and tomatoes. Serve with a good twist of black pepper.

SERVES 4

14 oz. canned lima beans, drained and rinsed

⅔ cup little gherkins or cornichons, finely chopped

1 red onion, finely sliced

large bunch of flat-leaf parsley, leaves picked

1 cup Canola Oil & English Mustard Dressing (*see* page 151), whisked with 1 extra tbsp English mustard powder

7 oz. Slow-braised Ham Hock (*see* page 154) or smoked ham, pulled into chunks

12 halves of Slow-roasted Tomatoes (*see* page 148)

freshly ground black pepper

Ham hock potato cakes
with minted peas, shallots, & parsley cream

If you are not braising your own ham hock (as on page 154), you can try buying it ready-cooked and shredded; otherwise, use some finely shredded smoked ham. In the summer, we serve these tasty potato cakes with a combination of warmed peas, cherry tomatoes, and mint in a lemon and olive oil dressing. During the winter, we go instead for this easy parsley sauce spiked with good old English mustard powder.

Preheat the oven to 390°F.

Bake the potatoes for 45 minutes, until a skewer shows no resistance when inserted. Cut them in half, scoop the flesh into a bowl, and discard the skins. Mash the potatoes, then mix with the egg, ham, capers, parsley, and lots of salt and pepper.

Put the semolina into a shallow bowl. With wet hands, divide the potato mixture into 8 equal pieces and shape into patties just under 1 in. thick. Coat lightly in the semolina and chill until ready to use.

Place the shallots in a roasting pan, drizzle with the oil, and season well. Roast for 15 minutes, until tender, then reduce the temperature to 280°F.

Meanwhile, place the peas, mint, and butter in a saucepan, season, and set aside. Put the mustard powder into another saucepan. Add a little of the cream and stir until smooth. Add the remaining cream and mix well. Set aside.

Heat 2 tablespoons of the olive oil in a large skillet and fry the potato cakes, a few at a time, for 2–3 minutes on each side, until golden. Place on a cookie sheet with the shallots and keep warm in the oven. Fry the remaining potato cakes in the same way.

Put the pan of peas over the heat and warm thoroughly. Similarly, warm the mustardy cream and stir in the parsley. When everything is ready, place 2 potato cakes onto each of 4 plates and pour the cream on top. Spoon over some peas and top with a few shallots.

SERVES 4

2 lb. 4 oz. russet potatoes, unpeeled

1 free-range egg

9 oz. Slow-braised Ham Hock (*see* page 154)

3 tbsp capers

4 tbsp flat-leaf parsley, chopped

salt and pepper

2 tbsp semolina, for coating

6 tbsp olive oil, for frying

For the shallots

7 oz. shallots, halved

2–3 tbsp extra virgin olive oil

For the peas

1 ½ cups frozen peas

sprig of mint

1 tbsp butter

For the parsley cream

1 tsp English mustard powder

5/8 cup heavy cream

3 tbsp flat-leaf parsley, chopped

Four types of puff pastry tartlets   EACH RECIPE MAKES 6

Here we have basic puff pastry bases with four different toppings, all of which are delicious warm or cold. These recipes offer a good way of using up leftovers, and the tarts are perfect for a light lunch or for taking on picnics. Using ready-rolled puff pastry takes out some of the elbow grease required.

Mushroom, feta cheese, & thyme

Preheat the oven to 390°F. Place the mushrooms in a baking sheet, drizzle with olive oil, season well, and roast for 15 minutes, until tender. Meanwhile, line a cookie sheet with nonstick parchment paper.

Cut the pastry into 5-in. squares and place them on the prepared cookie sheet. Place another cookie sheet directly on top and bake for 12–15 minutes, until the squares are crisp and pale golden but not risen.

Divide the mushrooms between the pastry squares. Top each one with 1 tablespoon of the feta cheese, a drizzle of oil, and a sprinkling of thyme leaves. Bake for an additional 5 minutes to warm through.

6 large or 12 small portobello mushrooms

olive oil, for drizzling

salt and pepper

11 oz. ready-rolled frozen puff pastry, defrosted overnight

3¼ oz. feta cheese, sliced

thyme leaves

Curly kale, blue cheese, & chili jam

Preheat the oven to 390°F.

Wash the kale and place it in a saucepan with just the residual water clinging to it and heat until wilted. Drain and roughly chop.

Place some kale on each baked pastry square and top with one sixth of the cheese and 2 teaspoons of chili jam. Warm in the oven for 5 minutes.

6 baked puff pastry squares (*see* method above)

14 oz. curly kale

5 oz. blue cheese

4 tbsp chili jam

Goat cheese, ham, & fig chutney

Preheat the oven to 390°F.

Spread each pastry square with 1 tablespoon of the chutney and sprinkle with one sixth of the goat cheese. Warm in the oven for 5 minutes.

Drape a slice of ham over the top and finish with a few arugula leaves and a good twist of black pepper.

6 baked puff pastry squares (*see method opposite*)

6 tbsp fig chutney

2 oz. goat cheese

6 slices of air-dried ham (we use cured ham, but prosciutto, speck, or Serrano ham will do)

arugula leaves, to serve

freshly ground black pepper

New potato, caramelized onion, & Brie

Heat the oil in a skillet. Add the potatoes, onion, and salt, then cover and cook over a low heat for 15 minutes, stirring occasionally, until completely soft. Allow to cool in the covered pan.

Preheat the oven to 390°F.

Spoon the potato mixture onto the baked pastry squares, add slices of Brie to each one, and warm in the oven for 5 minutes, until the cheese has melted.

Finish with a twist of black pepper, garnish with chopped parsley, and serve.

3 tbsp olive oil

10½ oz. new potatoes, sliced ¼ in. thick

1 white onion, thinly sliced

pinch of salt

6 baked puff pastry squares (*see method opposite*)

4 oz. Brie cheese, cut into slices

freshly ground black pepper

small bunch of flat-leaf parsley, leaves picked, to garnish

Mushroom & tarragon soup
with horseradish cream

In our busy kitchens, roasting mushrooms in the oven means that there's one less thing to stir on the crowded stove. At home you can, of course, cook them in a saucepan, but roasting does intensify their earthy flavor and brings out their sweetness. Adding sourdough bread crumbs to a mushroom soup gives it a lovely depth of flavor and also prevents it from separating. If you want a gluten-free version, omit the bread and add more mushrooms to compensate.

Preheat the oven to 390°F.

Put the mushrooms in a large roasting pan with the oil, garlic, salt, and pepper. Roast for 25–30 minutes, until tender and golden.

Meanwhile, make the horseradish cream. Mix the horseradish with the cream and lemon juice. Taste, adjust the lemon juice as necessary, and season to taste. Set aside.

Transfer the mushrooms to a saucepan, add the tarragon and bread crumbs, and heat for 5 minutes. Pour in the stock and bring to a simmer.

Puree the soup and loosen with water if you feel that it is too thick. Season well and add lemon juice to taste. Finish with the heavy cream.

Serve the soup in bowls and drizzle a little horseradish cream over the top.

SERVES 4–6

1 lb. 2 oz. brown or white mushrooms

4 tbsp extra virgin olive oil

2 large garlic cloves, chopped

salt and pepper

2 sprigs of tarragon, finely chopped

1 cup sourdough bread crumbs (made from crustless stale bread)

1 quart vegetable stock

juice of ½ lemon, or to taste

¼ cup heavy cream

For the horseradish cream

1 tbsp hot horseradish sauce or ½ tbsp grated fresh horseradish

⅔ cup heavy cream

dash of lemon juice

Parsnip & chestnut soup
with mustard butter

Sweet parsnips make a really satisfying soup. They need to be slowly sweated with butter to become fluffy and caramelized, so don't rush that part of the process. We like to use chicken stock to underpin the flavor of the soup, but if you want to keep it vegetarian, use vegetable stock instead.

Place the parsnips and butter in a large saucepan, cover, and cook over a very low heat for 30 minutes, stirring often, until soft and golden.

Add the chestnuts and honey and increase the heat until the chestnuts caramelize a little. Cover with the stock and simmer for an additional 20 minutes, until the chestnuts are really soft and will squash against the side of the pan when pressed with the back of a spoon.

Meanwhile, make the mustard butter. Melt the butter in a saucepan, then add the mustard and heat until it starts to smell fragrant and the seeds pop a little. Add the lemon juice and take off the heat.

Blend the soup to a puree, then return it to the pan and loosen it with a little water. Add the cream and season well with salt, pepper, and lemon juice.

Divide the soup between 4–6 bowls and drizzle each serving with a little of the mustard butter.

SERVES 4–6

3 lb. 5 oz. parsnips, peeled and thinly sliced

½ stick butter

7 oz. cooked peeled chestnuts

1 tbsp honey

1 quart chicken stock

½ cup heavy cream

salt and pepper

juice of ½ lemon

For the mustard butter

7 tbsp butter

1 tbsp whole-grain mustard

juice of ½ lemon

Cauliflower soup
with blue cheese & chutney

When cooked for a long time, cauliflower has a beautiful, velvety texture with a nutty and slightly spicy flavor. It goes excellently with blue cheese, but it needs some sharpness to stop the whole thing from getting too cloying, so we add lemon and a spoonful of chutney as a garnish.

Place the potatoes and onion in a large saucepan. Add the thyme and butter, cover, and cook over a low heat until the potato is tender and the onion is translucent. Add the garlic and cauliflower, stirring to coat in the butter, and cook for 5 minutes. Pour in the stock, cover, and simmer for 30 minutes, or until the cauliflower is tender.

Blend the soup to a smooth puree, then return it to the saucepan and loosen with a little water if necessary. Add the cream and heat through. Season well and add lemon juice to taste.

Set out your soup bowls. Crumble a little blue cheese or Stilton into each one, spoon the chutney on top, and pour the soup around it. Add a twist of black pepper on top and serve with slices of toasted granary bread.

SERVES 6

2 large potatoes, cubed

1 white onion, diced

sprig of thyme

3½ tbsp butter

2 garlic cloves, crushed

1 medium cauliflower (about 1 lb. 5 oz.), trimmed and broken into 1–1½-in. florets

1 quart vegetable stock

⅝ cup heavy cream

juice of ½ lemon

9 oz. blue cheese or Stilton cheese

4 tbsp chutney (we use pear or apple chutney)

freshly ground black pepper

slices of toasted granary bread, to serve

Spiced butternut squash & coconut soup

Sweet roasted butternut squash and spices are a culinary match made in heaven. Adding coconut milk really enriches the soup and tempers the flavors of the spices. Play around with how much chili you want to add, or serve with chili oil for drizzling if you are not sure how hot other people might like it.

Preheat the oven to 425°F.

Halve the squash and scoop out the seeds and discard. Place the squash in a large roasting pan.

Mix the oil with the garlic, cinnamon, fennel seeds, pepper flakes, and plenty of salt and pepper. Drizzle this mixture all over the squash, then cover with foil and roast for 45 minutes, until soft.

Scoop out the flesh of the squash from the skins and transfer it to a large saucepan. Cover with water, add the stock, and bring to a simmer.

Blend the soup to a smooth puree, then return it to the pan and loosen it with the coconut milk. Reheat and serve in soup bowls, drizzled with heavy cream and sprinkled with paprika. Offer chili oil at the table, for drizzling.

SERVES 6

2 large butternut squash

2 tbsp extra virgin olive oil

1 large garlic clove, crushed

1 tsp ground cinnamon

1 tsp fennel seeds

½ tsp red pepper flakes

salt and pepper

1⅔ cups vegetable stock

1⅔ cups canned coconut milk

To serve

heavy cream

paprika

chili oil, for drizzling

Roasted winter squash & pearl barley salad
with pumpkin seeds & dried cranberries

This is a really filling winter salad. Roasted squash is one of our favorite ingredients, but it does need to be lightly spiced and cooked to the point where it loses its starchiness and becomes sweet. If you want to try a variation, any other dried fruit will work, even some raisins.

Preheat the oven to 425°F.

Put the squash into a roasting pan, sprinkle with the olive oil, cinnamon, red pepper flakes, and seasoning, then toss well. Roast for 15 minutes, then turn, drizzle with the honey, and roast for an additional 10 minutes, until sweet, caramelized, and really tender, yet still holding its shape.

Meanwhile, put the pearl barley into a saucepan, cover with cold water, and bring to a boil. Simmer for about 35 minutes, until tender but with a little bite. Drain, allow to cool, then toss in 4 tablespoons of the dressing.

Spread the pearl barley in the bottom of a large, shallow serving dish. Cover with the roasted squash, then the cranberries. Combine all the leaves and arrange them over the top. Finally, sprinkle with the pumpkin seeds and drizzle with the remaining dressing.

SERVES 4

1 lb. 9 oz. butternut squash, peeled and cut into 1 ½-in. cubes
4 tbsp extra virgin olive oil
1 tsp ground cinnamon
1 tsp red pepper flakes
salt and pepper
2 tbsp honey
1 ½ cups pearl barley
⅝ cup Canola Oil & English Mustard Dressing (*see* page 151)
1 cup dried cranberries
3½ oz. baby spinach
3½ oz. arugula leaves
bunch of mint, roughly chopped
⅓ cup pumpkin seeds

Broccoli, sugar snap pea, & baby gem salad
with lemon-marinated feta cheese

This salad is a perennial favorite during the summer months, when we feel all the crunchy green vegetables are doing us so much good. It is a great salad to take on picnics, but don't refrigerate it or the oil will solidify and cling to the feta and the veggies will lose their flavor. Sugar snap peas, served raw when in season, are sweet and crunchy, but if those you find are not at their best, you might want to blanch them quickly first. Alternatively, throw in some fresh peas straight from the pod.

Cook the broccoli in a large pan of boiling, salted water for about 3 minutes, until tender but still crunchy. Drain in a colander, cool under cold running water, then shake dry.

Combine the oil and lemon zest in a bowl, then crumble in the feta cheese.

Cut each lettuce half into 4 wedges lengthwise. Place in a large bowl with the radishes, broccoli, sugar snap peas, and cucumber. Drizzle the dressing over everything and toss well.

Divide the salad between 4 bowls, placing the marinated feta cheese on top. Finish with a good twist of black pepper.

SERVES 4

11 oz. broccoli florets

salt and pepper

2 tbsp canola oil or olive oil

finely grated zest of 1 lemon

2 cups crumbled feta cheese

4 baby gem lettuces, halved lengthwise

8 radishes, thinly sliced

1 1/3 cups sugar snap peas, halved lengthwise

1/2 cucumber, thinly sliced

1/2 cup Canola Oil & English Mustard Dressing (*see* page 151)

Green lentil, beet, & red onion salad
with goat cheese

For this salad, we use a nonmatured British goat cheese, which has a fresh, tart flavor and no rind, and our mustardy dressing. It works well in both the summer and the winter. It's important that the lentils retain some bite, so be careful not to overcook them.

Preheat the oven to 390°F.

Put the beets in a saucepan of water and bring to a boil, then simmer for 30–45 minutes, until tender. Drain well, then rub off the skin and cut into quarters.

Meanwhile, cook the lentils in a pan of boiling water for 20–25 minutes, until tender but not slushy. Drain in a colander, hold under running water until cool, then drain again.

Place the lentils in a large bowl and stir in half the dressing. Add the parsley and top with the beets and onion. Sprinkle the cheese over the top, add a twist of black pepper, and serve with the remaining dressing on the side.

SERVES 4

9 beets, trimmed but unpeeled

1 ½ cups green lentils

1 cup Canola Oil & English Mustard Dressing (*see* page 151)

bunch of flat-leaf parsley, leaves picked

1 red onion, sliced

1 cup crumbled goat cheese

freshly ground black pepper

Warm red rice & chicken salad
with green beans & dates

The nutty flavor and satisfying bite of red rice make it ideal for a warm salad, and we almost always sell out of this particular one. On the rare occasions that there is some left at the end of the day, there's a fight over who gets to take it home. Note that olives can be used instead of dates and the chicken may be replaced with avocado to make the salad meat-free. Make sure you dress the rice while it's still warm so that it absorbs the flavors really well.

Preheat the oven to 360°F.

Put the chicken in a roasting pan, drizzle with the olive oil, and season generously with salt and pepper. Place in the oven and roast for 30–45 minutes. When cooked, skin and bone the chicken, then shred the meat.

Meanwhile, cook the rice in a pan of salted, boiling water for 25–30 minutes, until tender. Drain in a sieve, then transfer to a bowl and toss in the dressing while still warm. Add seasoning to taste, being fairly generous with salt, then stir in the herbs.

Blanch the beans in boiling water for 3–4 minutes, until tender. Add them to the rice, along with the dates and shredded chicken. Scatter with sliced almonds and serve.

SERVES 4

1 lb. 5 oz. chicken thighs

4 tbsp olive oil

salt and pepper

1 ⅓ cups red rice

1 cup Canola Oil & English Mustard Dressing (*see* page 151)

small bunch of flat-leaf parsley, leaves picked and roughly chopped

small bunch of mint, finely chopped

7 oz. green beans, topped

⅓ cup dates, cut into slivers

½ cup sliced almonds

Smoked mackerel pâté

This pâté is really easy to make—you just blend together all of the ingredients in the food processor—but make sure that you go for a hot horseradish sauce rather than a wimpy creamed type because it supplies the kick needed to cut through the oiliness of the fish.

Put all of the ingredients into a blender or food processor and blitz until smooth but not pureed—a maximum of 30 seconds, depending how good your blades are.

If serving later in the day, cover and chill, but take the pâté out of the refrigerator and allow it to come to room temperature before use.

Sprinkle the pâté with extra cayenne pepper and serve with slices of granary toast and a watercress salad.

SERVES 2

3 smoked mackerel fillets, skinned

4 tbsp crème fraîche or sour cream

1 ½ tbsp butter, softened

½ tbsp hot horseradish sauce

pinch of cayenne pepper

lemon juice, to taste

To serve

slices of granary toast

watercress salad

Smoked mackerel pâté club sandwich

Salty fish and crisp smoky bacon go beautifully together here. Note that the recipe above makes more pâté than the sandwiches require, but any leftovers are great as a snack.

Fry the bacon in the oil over a high heat until crisp. Keep warm. Toast the bread.

Take 2 slices of toast and spread each of them with 2 tablespoons of the pâté. Place 2 slices of bacon, 2 tomatoes and some lettuce on another 2 slices and sit these slices on top of the pâté slices so that you have 2 double-deckers.

Spread 1 tablespoon of mayonnaise on each slice of the remaining toast and place mayo-side down on the lettuce to make 2 triple-deckers. Cut in half diagonally and serve.

MAKES 2

4 slices of smoked Canadian bacon

1 tbsp sunflower oil

6 slices of granary farmhouse loaf, thinly sliced

4 tbsp Smoked Mackerel Pâté (*see* above)

4 Slow-roasted Tomatoes (*see* page 148)

iceberg lettuce, shredded

2 tbsp mayonnaise

Macaroni & cheese
with rosemary sourdough croutons

This dish can easily turn into a blobby mess if you overcook the pasta, so aim to have it just on the hard side of *al dente*. Make your cheese sauce slightly runnier than normal (just barely coating the back of a spoon) because pasta absorbs moisture and also dries out a little in the oven.

Preheat the oven to 425°F.

Cook the pasta in plenty of salted, boiling water for 1–2 minutes fewer than the instructions on the box, until barely *al dente*.

Meanwhile, make the cheese sauce. Melt the butter in a saucepan, add the flour, and cook for 1 minute, until smooth and bubbling. Take off the heat and gradually add the milk, stirring until smooth, then add the cream. Return to the heat and stir until very lightly coating the back of the spoon. Take off the heat again and add the cheeses, stirring until melted. Taste and season with salt and pepper.

Drain the pasta, return it to the saucepan, and stir in the sauce. Transfer to an ovenproof dish, sprinkle with the crushed croutons, and bake for 6–8 minutes, until bubbling around the edges.

SERVES 4

3¾ cups dried macaroni noodles

pinch of salt

2 handfuls of Rosemary Sourdough Croutons (*see* page 155), crushed

For the cheese sauce

½ stick butter

2 tbsp all-purpose flour

¾ cup whole milk

¾ cup heavy cream

½ cup grated Parmesan cheese

½ cup grated sharp cheddar cheese or Gruyère cheese

salt and pepper

Steak with Gentleman's Relish
& tarragon butter

I think we're a bit obsessed with Gentleman's Relish at Ginger & White. It's a salty little number made from anchovies and spices, and we offer it on the communal tables alongside our other condiments. When we opened in Belsize Park, north London, our first chef, Tom, came up with this magnificent butter and now we always keep some in the freezer. It's also great for slathering on roast beef sandwiches.

First, make the tarragon butter. Blitz the tarragon leaves in a food processor, then add the butter and Gentleman's Relish and blitz again. Roll the butter into a sausage, wrap in plastic wrap and store in the refrigerator.

Place a griddle pan over a high heat until really hot. Season the steaks with salt and pepper and brush with oil. Cook for 2 minutes on each side for medium rare or longer if you prefer your steak medium to well done. Take off the heat and allow to rest for 2 minutes.

Slice and top with a disk or two of the flavored butter. Serve with mixed lettuce leaves.

SERVES 2

2 x 9 oz. sirloin steaks

salt and pepper

olive oil

mixed lettuce leaves, to serve

For the tarragon butter

2 sprigs of tarragon, leaves only

1 stick butter, softened

1 tbsp Gentleman's Relish

Sandwiches

Goat cheese & baby spinach on crusty white
with red onion marmalade

A chunky white bread with crackled crust makes this sandwich out of this world, but granary or sourdough breads are good second bests. A very fresh, citrusy goat cheese—or, even better, goat curd—works well against the sweetness of the caramelized onions.

Cut the bread into 4 pieces, then cut each piece in half. Butter one half of each piece, top with the goat cheese, and spoon over the marmalade.

Finish with a small mound of baby spinach and a twist of black pepper. Cut in half and serve.

SERVES 4

1 large white bread loaf
1 ¾ tbsp butter, softened
7 oz. soft goat cheese or curd
2 tbsp red onion marmalade
1 oz. baby spinach
freshly ground black pepper

Brie, tomato, & baby basil on rye bread

We use a very malty, 100 percent rye bread for this sandwich, which pairs beautifully with delicious, creamy Brie. Look out for delicate leaves of baby basil if you can find it or just use torn basil leaves.

Put the tomatoes on a plate, drizzle with the oil, and season with salt and pepper.

Butter the bread. Put slices of Brie on 5 pieces of the bread. Top with 2 slices of tomato and sprinkle with the basil leaves. Top with the remaining bread. Cut in half and serve.

SERVES 5

2 tomatoes, each cut into 5 slices

1 tsp olive oil

salt and pepper

½ stick butter

10 slices of 100 percent rye bread

11 oz. Brie, sliced ½ in. thick

few sprigs of baby basil

Garlic & fennel slow-roasted pork buns
with apple sauce & garlic mayo

We serve these sandwiches at Hampstead's Christmas fair and also make them for Sunday lunches throughout the winter. Meltingly tender pork meat and crispy crackling are piled inside a soft bun with lashings of tart sauce or chutney. The pork itself is also good for a dinner dish served with stir-fried kale. Any leftovers can, of course, be used to fill the buns the next day.

Preheat the oven to 300°F.

Turn the pork skin-side down and make small slits all over the flesh. Slot the garlic into the slits, then sprinkle with red pepper flakes, half the fennel seeds, and the salt.

Place the joint in a deep roasting pan, skin-side up, and dry the skin with paper towel. Smear with the oil and the remaining fennel seeds. Roast in the oven for 4 hours. If the skin does not produce good crackling, carefully slice it off and place under a medium-hot broiler until it blisters. Meanwhile, pull the meat apart with 2 forks.

Spread the garlic mayo on one half of each bun; butter the other half and smear it with apple sauce. Pile some pork and crackling on the base of each bun, sandwich together, and serve immediately.

MAKES 8

4-lb. pork shoulder, rolled and boned, skin scored

3 garlic cloves, thickly sliced

1 tsp red pepper flakes

1 tbsp fennel seeds

1 tbsp salt

2 tbsp extra virgin olive oil

1 cup Roasted Garlic Mayonnaise (*see* page 150)

8 soft white buns, cut in half

1 stick butter, softened

¾ cup McIntosh Apple Sauce (*see* page 157) or rhubarb chutney

Pulled ham hock on potato sourdough
with roasted mustardy shallots

Our sandwiches are made with a lot of love and the very best British ingredients—from artisan breads and cheeses to chutneys and free-range meats. We try very hard to devise original flavor combinations, and this one was created for us by Scott, one of our chefs. Slow-braised ham hock (also known as pork knuckle) is so different to sliced ham—it offers extra pillowy softness as well as a salty, smoky flavor. The chefs who make this sandwich often end up with yellow hands from the turmeric in the mustardy shallots.

Preheat the oven to 320°F.

First make the mustardy shallots. Combine the mustard seeds, turmeric, and mustard powder in a roasting pan and mix in the oil. Add the shallots and toss well. Roast for 30–40 minutes, until soft but not browned, and the spices are thoroughly cooked.

Cut the loaf into quarters, slice each quarter in half, and butter each half. Pile the ham on the bottom slices of each sourdough quarter, top with the shallots, and sprinkle with the parsley. Top with the remaining bread and serve.

SERVES 4

1 potato sourdough ring

½ stick butter, softened

½ lb. Slow-braised Ham Hock (*see* page 154), shredded

handful of flat-leaf parsley leaves

For the mustardy shallots

½ tsp yellow mustard seeds

½ tsp ground turmeric

1 tsp English mustard powder

2 tbsp olive oil

2 large shallots or small white onions, cut into wedges through the root

Coronation chicken sandwich

Coronation chicken was created in Britain for Queen Elizabeth's coronation in 1953. Lighten the mayonnaise in the chicken mixture by adding some yogurt and sharp chutney. If using a korma paste that has already had its spices cooked out, simply stir all the ingredients together. The chicken filling is also delicious served at room temperature on hot white toast.

Put the chicken in a bowl with the yogurt, mayonnaise, korma paste, and chutney and mix well. Season with salt and pepper, then taste and add the honey if the flavor is too sharp.

Butter 4 slices of the bread. Place about 4 tablespoons of the chicken mixture on each piece, then top with some of the lettuce and the other slices of bread. Cut in half and serve.

MAKES 4

13 oz. cooked chicken, shredded

¼ cup plain yogurt

¼ cup mayonnaise

2 tbsp korma paste

2 tbsp mango or apricot and ginger chutney

salt and pepper

1 tbsp clear honey (optional)

1 ¾ tbsp butter, softened

8 slices of white bloomer bread

iceberg or baby gem lettuce, shredded

Roast chicken, bacon, & caper mayo bun

A good chicken sandwich needs plenty of mayonnaise spiked with English mustard, capers, and cornichons. It's a great way to use up the remains of a roast chicken dinner, and the mayo also works really well with salami or smoked salmon sandwiches.

Place the chicken in a bowl, add the caper mayonnaise, and stir well.

Fry the bacon in a skillet until crisp.

Slice the buns in half, butter them, and pile the chicken mixture on one half. Add a handful of radicchio and a slice of bacon to each. Top with the remaining bun halves and serve.

MAKES 6

1 lb. 5 oz. cooked chicken, shredded

¼ cup Caper Mayonnaise (*see* page 150)

6 slices of smoked Canadian bacon

6 white sandwich buns

2 tbsp butter, softened

½ head of radicchio, leaves torn

Corned beef on sourdough
with cucumber pickles & mustard mayo

We slowly braise our own corned beef using brisket and spices to make a really tender, slightly sticky filling for this classic sandwich. It is also worth making your own pickles instead of buying them because the store-bought ones are often pretty acidic. If you prefer not to toast the bread (though the sandwich really is more delicious that way), omit the cheese—it somehow seems like overkill on fresh bread.

Put the mayonnaise and mustard powder into a bowl and mix together until combined.

Butter the bread slices and spread the mustard mayo on half of the buttered slices. Layer the beef, cheese, and pickles on the slices with the mayo and top with the remaining buttered bread.

Toast the sandwiches in batches in a panini grill or a medium-hot skillet until the cheese has melted and the bread is lightly toasted. Cut in half and serve immediately, with a side of fries or potato wedges, if desired.

MAKES 4

4 tbsp mayonnaise

1 tsp English mustard powder

3 tbsp butter, softened

8 slices of sourdough bloomer

7 oz. Braised Corned Beef (*see* page 153), thinly sliced

2 oz. sharp cheddar cheese, sliced

12 Cucumber Pickles (*see* page 153)

fries or potato wedges, to serve (optional)

Chorizo & tomato on ciabatta
with caper mayo

We use a British chorizo supplier called Bath Pig for this sandwich. The caper mayo cuts through the richness of the chorizo, while making the chewy ciabatta deliciously moist.

Open the loaf and butter the bottom half. Spread with the caper mayonnaise. Cover with the chorizo, tomatoes, and watercress, then add a twist of black pepper.

Sandwich the bread together then cut into 4 and serve.

MAKES 4

1 ciabatta or potato sourdough loaf, cut in half horizontally

1 ¾ tbsp butter, softened

5 ½ tbsp Caper Mayonnaise (*see* page 150)

20 thin slices of chorizo

2 plum tomatoes, thinly sliced

handful of watercress

freshly ground black pepper

Fish stick, lettuce, & tartare sauce sandwich

It seems like every British menu these days is offering a fish stick sandwich, but when we first opened in Hampstead, this was still very much a guilty pleasure. You need fresh, white, squashy bread—it cannot be a day old—and the fish sticks are much better if deep-fried. We think that the uniform frozen fish sticks you buy in a store are better in a sandwich than homemade ones, and we're not ashamed to admit it.

Fill a deep-fat fryer with oil and heat to 350°F, or preheat the oven to 400°F and put a lightly oiled baking sheet inside to heat.

Deep-fry the fish sticks for 3–4 minutes or bake them in the oven for 10–12 minutes, until golden.

Meanwhile, butter 2 slices of the bread and spread the other 2 slices with tartare sauce. Put the fish sticks and lettuce on the saucy side, cover with the remaining bread, then slice in half, and serve with a side of fries or potato wedges, if desired.

MAKES 2

oil, for deep-frying or greasing

8 good-quality fish sticks

1 ½ tbsp butter

4 slices of soft white bread

4 tbsp tartare sauce

1 baby gem lettuce, leaves separated

fries or potato wedges, to serve (optional)

Baking

Savory muffins

Arriving at work one morning, hungover and dying for a greasy breakfast, our first chef, Jess, came up with this savory treat instead. Her first batch sold out in an hour, and we've never looked back. We fill these muffins with anything and everything, although beware—using high-moisture ingredients, such as spinach or tomatoes, can make them soggy, so if you want to include these ingredients, mix them half-and-half with something drier, such as cheese or ham.

Preheat the oven to 400°F. Set out a 6-hole silicone muffin pan, or line a metal muffin pan with paper cups.

Place the buttermilk, or mixture of yogurt and milk, in a bowl with the oil. Mix with a fork, then whisk in the egg.

Put all the dry ingredients into another bowl and add the egg mixture, stirring well to make sure that there are no dry, floury pockets (it can be a little lumpy). Don't overwork the mixture.

Fold in whatever savory ingredients you're using, reserving some for decoration. Spoon the mixture into the holes of the muffin pan, almost to the top of each hole. Place the reserved savory ingredients on top so that you can later see what's inside the muffin. Bake for 25–30 minutes, until golden brown.

Gently turn the pan upside down on a dishtowel and ease out the muffins. Place them upside down on a wire rack to cool (the muffins are top-heavy, so doing this prevents the lighter part underneath from getting squashed). Turn them the right way up once cooled.

MAKES 6

⅔ cup buttermilk, or ¼ cup plain yogurt plus 3⅓ tbsp whole milk
4 tbsp extra virgin olive oil
1 free-range egg
1½ cups all-purpose flour
¼ tsp baking soda
1 tsp baking powder
1 tbsp superfine sugar
½ tsp sea salt
⅔–1 cup savory ingredients (see Fillings, opposite)

FILLINGS

Marmite, cheddar, & ham muffins:
Whisk ½ tablespoon Marmite into the batter, then fold in ¼ cup grated sharp cheddar or American cheese and 1½ oz chopped smoked ham. After baking, grate another ⅛ cup cheddar, sprinkle a little on each muffin, and return to the oven for 2 minutes, until melted.

Tomato, feta, & thyme muffins:
Add ¼ cup chopped Slow-roasted Tomatoes (*see* page 148) to the batter, then fold in ¼ cup crumbled feta and the leaves from a sprig of thyme. Spoon into the holes of the muffin pan, then crumble a little extra feta cheese over each muffin and sprinkle with a few thyme leaves before baking.

Bacon, Parmesan, & scallion muffins:
Add 2 slices of chopped cooked Canadian bacon to the batter, then fold in ¼ cup grated Parmesan cheese and 6 chopped scallions. After baking, sprinkle a little more grated Parmesan on each muffin and return to the oven for 2 minutes, until melted.

Chorizo, black olive, & chili muffins:
Fold 2½ oz. chopped chorizo, 1 oz. finely chopped pitted black olives, and ¼ teaspoon red pepper flakes into the batter. Bake as opposite.

Gluten-free almond & pistachio cake

This is quite a modern cake for us, but it sums up our view of London. It is a melting pot of flavors and ideas—slightly Italian and a bit Middle Eastern with a G&W twist. Our interest in gluten-free cooking was kicked off when Tonia's daughter Lily Lois was diagnosed with celiac disease. Since then, we generally try to avoid having gluten in our cakes, which is actually easier than you might think. We don't see why anyone should have to miss out—especially when it comes to cake!

Preheat the oven to 360°F. Lightly grease a 2-lb. bread pan and line the base with nonstick parchment paper.

Put the butter and sugar into a bowl and beat together until pale and fluffy. Add the eggs a little at a time, beating in each addition until fully incorporated. Stir in all of the ground nuts, the flour, and lemon zest.

Spoon the mixture into the prepared pan and bake for about 45 minutes, until a skewer inserted into the center of the cake comes out clean. Set aside to cool in the pan.

Meanwhile, make the topping. Heat the sugar and lemon juice in a saucepan. When the sugar has totally dissolved, stir in the rosewater and pistachios, then pour the mixture evenly over the cake. Leave to cool completely, then turn out of the pan, cut into slices, and serve.

SERVES 8–10

2½ sticks unsalted butter, plus extra for greasing

1 cup superfine sugar

4 free-range eggs, beaten

⅔ cup ground almonds

½ cup ground pistachios

¼ cup gluten-free, all-purpose flour

finely grated zest of 2 unwaxed lemons

For the topping

⅓ cup superfine sugar

juice of 2 lemons

1 drop of rosewater

½ cup pistachios, chopped

Orange & almond tray bake
with orange flower water syrup

This unconventional cake recipe asks you to boil whole unpeeled oranges and then simply mix them with sugar and ground almonds. This method crops up in many sources, but Tonia first discovered it in Claudia Roden's *Mediterranean Cookery*. When they met at an event, Claudia acknowledged that it was in fact someone else's recipe, so it just goes to show how ideas get passed around and no one can ever truly claim ownership.

Place the oranges in a saucepan, cover with water, and bring to a boil. (They will bob around on the surface, so don't worry that they are not submerged.) Simmer, uncovered, for 2 hours, until very soft and squashy. Drain the fruit and set aside to cool.

Preheat the oven to 360°F. Grease the sides of a 12 × 16-in. baking pan and line the base with nonstick parchment paper.

Cut the oranges into quarters and remove any seeds. Blitz the quarters, skin and all, in a blender or food processor until you have a smooth puree.

Whisk the eggs in a large bowl, then beat in the sugar, ground almonds, and baking powder. Fold in the orange puree, then pour the mixture into the prepared pan. Bake for 35 minutes, until a skewer inserted in the center comes out clean.

Meanwhile, make the syrup and decoration. Place the sugar and water in a saucepan over a low heat until the sugar has dissolved: do not stir. Add the orange slices and simmer for 10 minutes, until soft. Remove the slices from the syrup with a slotted spoon and dry on nonstick parchment paper. Add the orange flower water to the syrup and set aside.

Allow the cake to cool in the pan, then cut into 8 squares. Drizzle with the syrup, then decorate each square with a slice of candied orange and a raspberry.

SERVES 8

2 oranges
softened butter, for greasing
6 free-range eggs
1 ¼ cups superfine sugar
1 ¼ cups ground almonds
½ tsp baking powder

For the syrup & decoration

⁴⁄₅ cup superfine sugar
⁴⁄₅ cup water
1 orange, thinly sliced
2 drops of orange flower water
8 raspberries

Dark chocolate brownie bites

We find that sometimes a whole brownie is just too much, so we had a brainwave: cut them into bite-size pieces and you've got the perfect portion (which we then eat five of!). We must also mention the mini Stonehenge replica our manager Bosun creates with these tasty morsels.

Preheat the oven to 400°F. Line a 9-in. square baking pan with nonstick parchment paper, or use a 9-in. silicone pan.

Place the butter and dark chocolate in a heatproof bowl set over a saucepan of simmering water over a low heat and stir until just smooth. Allow to cool.

Place the eggs and the sugar in a bowl and beat until light and creamy. Using a spatula or a large metal spoon, fold in the chocolate mixture. Sift over the flour and cocoa powder and mix to combine. Add the chocolate chunks or chips, then pour the mixture into the prepared pan.

Bake for 35–40 minutes, until just set in the middle. You cannot use a skewer to test brownies for readiness, as they will always be moist. They will firm up after cooling, so always err on the side of cooking them less. When cool, cut into 20 bite-size pieces.

MAKES 20

2¼ sticks butter

9 oz. dark chocolate (at least 70 percent cocoa solids), broken into pieces

4 free-range eggs

2 cups unrefined superfine sugar

1 cup all-purpose flour

1 cup cocoa powder

4½ oz. milk or dark chocolate, roughly chopped, or 1 cup white chocolate chips

Vanilla cupcakes

It seems that everywhere you look these days, someone is making cupcakes, but when we first started making them in Hampstead, there was nowhere local to buy them. Some of our bakers love making them as lurid as possible (our younger clientele tend to choose these), while others prefer more pastel hues. We use a 2-D tip to get a pretty rose effect on top.

Preheat the oven to 400°F. Set out 2 cupcake pans and line with paper bake cups.

Whisk the eggs and sugar in a bowl until pale and foamy. Sift in the flour, salt, and baking powder and whisk again. Pour in the cream, melted butter, and vanilla extract and whisk again.

Spoon the batter into the paper cups so that they are two thirds full. Bake for 22–25 minutes, until a skewer inserted in the center of one of the cakes comes out clean. The cakes should be quite pale, rather than golden. Allow to cool for 15 minutes, then transfer to a wire rack and leave until completely cooled.

Make the frosting as instructed on page 156, but add the food coloring and beat until evenly distributed before folding in the cream cheese.

Spoon the frosting into a pastry bag fitted with a 2-D tip (*see* tip, below). Gently squeezing the bag and starting in the middle of each cupcake, pipe the frosting in circles until the top is covered. To decorate, scatter with sprinkles or dot a few candies on top.

MAKES 18

4 free-range eggs
1¾ cups superfine sugar
2½ cups all-purpose flour
¼ tsp fine salt
1 tsp baking powder
½ cup heavy cream
1 stick unsalted butter, melted
1 tsp vanilla extract
sprinkles or little candies, for decorating

For the frosting

1 quantity Cream Cheese Frosting (*see* page 156)
1 drop of food coloring (tiny for pastel frosting; bigger for a lurid effect)

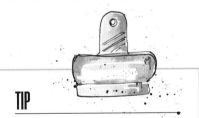

TIP

An easy way to fill a pastry bag is to place it in a pitcher and fold about 3 in. of the bag over the edge. This keeps it open and steady while you spoon in the frosting.

Mini chocolate cupcakes

Delicate swirls of frosting covered in little star sprinkles make these cupcakes look magical. We like to pipe it on with the same-size 2-D tip as for the larger ones (available from cake craft stores), but you can spread it with a spatula if you prefer. To go all out on the chocolate front, we may add chocolate shavings. Although small, they offer all the flavor of bigger cupcakes, but with only a fraction of the naughtiness.

Preheat the oven to 400°F. Set out 2 mini cupcake pans and line them with paper bake cups.

Whisk the eggs and sugar in a bowl until pale and foamy. Sift in the flour, cocoa powder, salt, and baking powder and whisk again. Pour in the cream and melted butter and whisk until just combined.

Spoon the batter into the paper cups so that they are two thirds full. Bake for 12–15 minutes, or until a skewer inserted in the center of one of the cakes comes out clean. Allow to cool for 15 minutes, then transfer to a wire rack and leave until completely cooled.

To make the frosting, put the butter into a bowl and beat until pale and fluffy. Sift in the powdered sugar and cocoa powder and beat again until smooth. Finally, fold in the cream cheese—don't overbeat the frosting at this stage or it might become too soft.

Spoon the frosting into a pastry bag fitted with a 2-D tip (*see* tip, opposite). Gently squeezing the bag and starting in the middle of each cupcake, pipe the frosting in circles until the top is covered. To decorate, scatter with mini sprinkles.

MAKES 16

2 free-range eggs

⁴⁄₅ cup superfine sugar

1 cup all-purpose flour

4½ tbsp cocoa powder

2 pinches of fine salt

½ tsp baking powder

¼ cup heavy cream

½ stick unsalted butter, melted

mini star sprinkles

For the frosting

1 stick unsalted butter, softened

1⅔ cups powdered sugar

1 tbsp cocoa powder

¼ cup full-fat cream cheese

Mini gooseberry & elderflower sponge cakes

A world away from the stuffy old tearoom selection, this is cool baking, Ginger & White style. We've swapped traditional strawberry jam for the zingy taste of gooseberry and elderflower, and we've shrunk the cakes because we believe good things come in the smallest packages.

Preheat the oven to 400°F and place a shelf in the center of it. Grease the 12 holes of a muffin pan.

Put the butter and sugar into a bowl and beat until pale and fluffy. Beat in the eggs one at a time, then add the elderflower syrup. Sift in the flour and gently fold together using a large metal spoon. The mixture should drop off the end of the spoon when tapped; if it doesn't, add enough of the milk until it does.

Spoon 2 tablespoons of the mixture into each hole of the prepared muffin pan. Bake for 10–15 minutes, until springy to the touch.

Meanwhile, make the filling. Beat the butter until pale and fluffy. Sift in the powdered sugar and beat again until smooth, scraping down the sides with a spatula to make sure that the mixture is thoroughly combined. Finally, fold in the cream cheese—don't overbeat the filling at this stage or it might become too soft.

Allow the cakes to cool in the pan for 5 minutes, then transfer to a wire rack and leave until completely cold.

To serve, cut each cake in half horizontally. Spread the filling on the bottom half and gooseberry jam on the top half. Sandwich together and dust with superfine sugar.

MAKES 12

sunflower oil, for greasing

2 sticks unsalted butter, softened

1 cup superfine sugar

4 free-range eggs

4 tbsp elderflower syrup

1¾ cups self-rising flour

1–2 tbsp whole milk (optional)

¾ cup gooseberry jam

superfine sugar, for dusting

For the filling

1 stick unsalted butter, softened

1½ cups powdered sugar

3 tbsp cream cheese

Ginger & White carrot cake

We're not going to lie: it took us months to nail this recipe. The perfect carrot cake is busy, but not so packed with nuts, raisins, and carrots that you can't taste the delicious cake holding it all together. And as for the luscious frosting—that's why we always eat from the top down.

Preheat the oven to 360°F. Grease the sides of 2 × 9-in. springform cake pans and line the bases with disks of nonstick parchment paper.

Sift the flour, baking powder, baking soda, cinnamon, pumpkin pie mix, and salt into a large mixing bowl and stir together.

Separate 2 of the eggs. Break the 2 whole eggs into the bowl containing the separated egg yolks, add the sugar and oil, and beat until combined. Stir in the carrots, then fold in the raisins and walnuts. Lightly fold in the dry ingredients using a large metal spoon or spatula.

Whisk the egg whites until softly peaking. Fold half of them into the flour mixture, then fold in the remainder, keeping as much air as possible in the mixture.

Divide the batter evenly between the prepared pans and bake for 45 minutes in the center of the oven. When ready, a skewer inserted into the center of the cakes should come out clean. Allow to cool in the pans, then turn out onto a wire rack and allow to cool completely.

To make the frosting, put the butter into a bowl and beat until pale and fluffy. Sift in the powdered sugar and beat again until smooth. Finally, beat in the cream cheese, but don't overbeat it or it might become grainy.

Using a spatula, spread frosting on one half of the cake. Sit the other half on top, then frost the sides and top. Place the walnut halves in a circle on the frosting to mark out the portions.

SERVES 12

1 ¼ cups sunflower oil, plus extra for greasing

2⅘ cups all-purpose flour

2 tsp baking powder

½ tsp baking soda

1 tsp ground cinnamon

1 tsp pumpkin pie mix

¼ tsp fine salt

4 free-range eggs

2¼ cups unrefined superfine sugar

11 oz carrots, grated

⅔ cup raisins

1 cup walnuts, chopped, plus 12 walnut halves for decoration

For the frosting

2⅓ sticks unsalted butter, softened

2½ cups powdered sugar

2½ cups full-fat cream cheese

Rhubarb & almond crumble cake

Crunchy crumble, buttery sponge cake, and tart fruit are a winning combination. We change the fruit in this cake according to the seasons, using forced rhubarb during the winter, blackberries and raspberries in the summer, gooseberries in the spring, and apples in the fall.

Preheat the oven to 360°F. Grease an 8-in. round springform cake pan and line the base with a disk of nonstick parchment paper.

Cream the butter and sugar together in a bowl until pale and fluffy. Beat in the eggs and vanilla extract a little at a time, then fold in the flour, baking powder, baking soda, and ground almonds. Beat in the sour cream or plain yogurt until the mixture drops off the spoon slowly, then pour half of it into the prepared pan. Arrange the sliced rhubarb on top, then cover with the remaining cake batter.

To make the crumble topping, put the flour, sugar, and cinnamon into a bowl, add the butter, and blend with your fingertips until the mixture is crumbly. Add the water and the sliced almonds and mix together with a blunt knife. Scatter the lumpy mixture over the cake and bake for 50–60 minutes.

To check for readiness, insert a skewer into the center of the cake; if it doesn't come out clean, allow to bake for a few minutes more before checking again (remember, the fruit will make it a bit wetter than a regular cake). Allow to cool in the pan for 10 minutes, then transfer to a wire rack until just warm or completely cold. Serve slices of cake, with cream drizzled over the top, if desired.

SERVES 8

2 sticks unsalted butter, softened, plus extra for greasing

1 ⅛ cups superfine sugar

3 free-range eggs, beaten

3 tsp vanilla extract

1 ¼ cups all-purpose flour

1 tsp baking powder

½ tsp baking soda

¾ cup ground almonds

⅔ cup sour cream or plain yogurt

11 oz. forced rhubarb, very thinly sliced

heavy cream, to serve (optional)

For the crumble topping

½ cup all-purpose flour

½ cup light brown sugar

½ tsp ground cinnamon

½ stick unsalted butter, softened

1 tbsp water

1 ¼ cups sliced almonds

Gluten-free lemon & raspberry loaves

Semolina adds a crunchy bite to cakes and is gluten-free. We make these in mini bread pans, but a large bread pan can be used instead. Zigzag frosting drizzled on top looks great, and, if serving immediately, fresh raspberries or strawberries give a summery twist.

Preheat the oven to 360°F. Grease 12 mini bread pans or line the base of a 2-lb. bread pan with nonstick parchment paper.

Place the butter, sugar, and lemon zest in a bowl and beat until really light and fluffy. Now beat in the eggs a little at a time. If the mixture looks curdled, add a tablespoon of the flour. Fold in the remaining flour, the semolina, ground almonds, and lemon juice.

Spoon the mixture into the prepared pans and bake for 18–22 minutes, until well risen and a skewer inserted into the center of one of them comes out clean. (If using a large pan, bake for 50 minutes and then do the skewer test.) Remove from the oven and allow to cool in the pan(s) for 15 minutes. Transfer to a wire rack and leave until completely cool.

For the lemon frosting, mix the powdered sugar with a drop of lemon juice and stir energetically until smooth. The frosting should be thin but should hold its own weight and drizzle in nice fluid lines. We test this on a saucer first. If too thick, add more juice. Using a spoon or a plastic bag snipped at one corner, zigzag the frosting over the loaves. Sprinkle with the raspberries and serve.

MAKES 12

2¼ sticks unsalted butter, softened, plus extra for greasing

1¼ cups superfine sugar

finely grated zest and juice of 1 lemon

4 free-range eggs, beaten

⅓ cup gluten-free self-rising flour, sifted

¾ cup fine semolina

⅜ cup ground almonds

dried or fresh raspberries, to decorate

For the lemon frosting

1¼ cups powdered sugar

lemon juice

Caramel croissant bread & butter "puddings"

Getting the caramel really dark for this recipe requires a bit of bravery, but it pays off as the sweetness is balanced by an almost burned tang. We usually make individual bread and butter puddings in silicone muffin pans, but you can just as easily put the mixture into a single large ovenproof dish. In either case, the pudding should be a little wobbly in the middle when removed from the oven because it sets as it cools.

First make the caramel. Place the sugar and the water in a saucepan and, without stirring, bring to a simmer over a low heat (stirring encourages crystals to form). When the sugar has dissolved, increase the heat and let the mixture become deep brown. Be brave and wait until it is just about to smoke and burn, then take the pan off the heat and carefully pour in the cream—this might hiss and splutter as it hits the caramel. Return the pan to the heat and stir the mixture until smooth. Set aside to cool at room temperature. When cool enough to handle, pour into a pitcher.

Meanwhile, make the custard. Whisk the cream, milk, and eggs together until combined, then strain into a separate pitcher.

Grease a 6-hole muffin pan or use a silicone muffin pan. Place the ugly croissant ends in the holes, then arrange the neat slices on top so that they protrude a bit above the pan. Pour over the caramel, reserving ½ cup for later. Pour the custard over the top and place the puddings in the fridge to soak for 1 hour.

Preheat the oven to 360°F. Pour hot water into a large roasting pan to a depth of about 1 in. Place the muffin pan in the water and bake the puddings for 25–35 minutes, until just set in the center. Set aside to cool for 5–10 minutes. Drizzle the remaining caramel over the puddings and sprinkle with the walnuts. Lift out with a blunt knife and transfer to serving plates.

MAKES 6

softened butter, for greasing

6 croissants, cut widthwise into slices around 1 in. thick

3 tbsp chopped toasted walnuts

For the caramel

1 ¼ cups granulated or superfine sugar

4 tbsp water

½ cup heavy cream

For the custard

⅘ cup heavy cream

⅔ cup whole milk

2 free-range eggs, plus 2 yolks

Ginger & White scones

Remember to be light with your hands when making scones—it's important not to overwork the flour and butter. When it comes to stamping them out, make sure they're over 1 in. high. If not, your scones will be sad, flat little things, and that's no fun at all.

Preheat the oven to 425°F. Lightly oil a cookie sheet and dust with a little flour.

Put the flour, baking powder, butter, and salt into a large bowl and pulse in a food processor or blend with your fingertips until the mixture resembles coarse bread crumbs.

In a separate bowl, whisk the egg with only ⅓ cup of the milk using a fork.

Fold the sugar into the flour mixture, then stir in the whisked milk mixture. The aim is to create a soft dough that's not wet or sticky. If it seems dry, trickle in a little more milk to reach the right consistency.

Place the dough on a work surface lightly dusted with flour. Using a floured rolling pin, roll out the dough to a thickness of 1 in. Dip a 2-in. cutter in a little extra flour to prevent it from sticking and stamp out 5 circles, dipping again between each cut. For quirky, lopsided scones that have a certain charm of their own, twist the cutter as you stamp them out.

Reroll the offcuts—you should be able to get another 1 or 2 scones out of them. Place the scones on the prepared cookie sheet and brush the tops with milk. Bake for 12–15 minutes, until lightly golden and risen. When done, they'll sound hollow when tapped. Transfer the scones to a wire rack to cool.

Serve the scones with generous amounts of whipped cream and strawberry jam.

MAKES 7

sunflower oil, for greasing

1 ¾ cups self-rising flour

1 tsp baking powder

½ stick unsalted butter, cubed

pinch of salt

1 large free-range egg

½ cup whole milk, plus extra for glazing

2½ tbsp superfine sugar

To serve

good-quality whipping cream, whipped

strawberry jam

Gluten-free marmalade loaf
with cardamom glaze

If Paddington Bear were coming for a tea party, this is what we'd serve him. Marmalade offers the perfect balance of sweet and tart flavors, and, unlike with a lot of gluten-free cooking, this cake doesn't have a ground almond in sight, which therefore makes it suitable for those with nut allergies. We find that using a tawny Seville orange marmalade makes all the difference to the flavor.

Preheat the oven to 360°F. Grease a 2-lb. bread pan and line the base with nonstick parchment paper.

To make the glaze, place all the ingredients in a pan and bring to a boil, then set the liquid aside to infuse.

Meanwhile, cream together the butter and sugar in a bowl until pale and fluffy. Beat in the orange zest and then the marmalade. Gradually beat in the eggs a little at a time, then fold in the flour.

Spoon the mixture into the prepared pan and bake for 40–55 minutes, or until the loaf is pale golden and a skewer inserted into the middle comes out clean. Remove from the oven and allow to cool in the pan for 15 minutes. When cold, lift out using a blunt knife and transfer to a wire rack.

To decorate, mix the powdered sugar with a drop of orange juice and stir energetically until smooth. If too thick, add more juice.

Using a spoon or a plastic bag snipped at one corner, zigzag the frosting over the loaf. Drizzle with the glaze and slice to serve.

SERVES 9

1 ½ sticks unsalted butter, softened, plus extra for greasing

½ cup superfine sugar

finely grated zest of 1 orange

⅓ cup tawny Seville orange marmalade

3 free-range eggs, beaten

1 ⅓ cups gluten-free self-rising flour

For the glaze

scant ⅓ cup tawny Seville orange marmalade

juice of 1 orange

seeds from 6 cardamom pods

For the frosting

1 ¼ cups powdered sugar

orange juice

Lemon curd layer cake

Humor us while we get nostalgic—lemon curd on white bread is the taste of our childhood. Now that we're all grown up, this lemon curd cake is how we take a stroll down memory lane. The curd can be heated in an ordinary saucepan—there's no need to put it over a bain-marie or double boiler—which makes things much quicker.

Start by making the curd filling. Put the egg yolks and sugar in a small, heavy-based saucepan and beat with a wooden spoon until smooth. Beat in the lemon zest, juice, and butter, then place over a low heat for 5–10 minutes, stirring constantly until thick. Allow to cool, then cover and chill until needed.

Preheat the oven to 360°F. Grease 3 × 9-in. diameter springform cake pans and line the bases with nonstick parchment paper.

Place the butter, sugar, and lemon zest in a bowl and beat until really light and fluffy. Beat in the eggs a little at a time. If the mixture looks curdled, add 1 tablespoon of the flour. Finally, fold in the remaining flour. You will be left with a really thick mixture, but don't be tempted to add any liquid.

Spoon the mixture into the prepared pans and smooth out the top. Bake for 12–15 minutes, until the cakes are shrinking away from the sides of the pans and a skewer inserted in the center comes out clean.

Turn out the cakes onto a wire rack, peel off the paper and allow to cool. When cool, spread 1 sponge with half the lemon curd, place another sponge upside down on top, and spread the remaining curd on that. Top with the final sponge cake, dust with powdered sugar, and decorate with fresh strawberries or blueberries.

SERVES 8

2 sticks unsalted butter, softened, plus extra for greasing

1 ⅛ cups superfine sugar

finely grated zest of 2 lemons

4 free-range eggs at room temperature, beaten

1 ¾ cups self-rising flour

powdered sugar, for dusting

strawberries or blueberries, for decoration

For the curd filling

3 large free-range egg yolks

½ cup superfine sugar

finely grated zest of 3 lemons and ⅓ cup lemon juice

½ stick unsalted butter

Stem ginger loaf
with vanilla frosting

Here we have a dark, brooding mother of a cake, full of strong, spicy flavors that balance the sweetness of the frosting. The little chunks of stem ginger make it stand out from the crowd, so this recipe is definitely one to impress. The high sugar content means that it is prone to getting too dark, so if you notice it turning black after 30 minutes, turn down the oven to 320°F.

Preheat the oven to 360°F. Grease a 2-lb. bread pan and line the bottom with nonstick parchment paper.

Put the water into a saucepan and bring to a boil. Add the butter, sugar, molasses, and syrup and heat gently, stirring to combine, until just melted. Set aside to cool for 20 minutes, then stir in the chopped ginger and its syrup, followed by the eggs.

Sift together the flour, spices, and salt. Add to the syrup mixture and fold together.

Spoon the batter into the prepared pan and bake for 55–60 minutes, until a skewer inserted into the center comes out clean. Allow to cool in the pan, then loosen the sides with a spatula, turn upside down onto a dishtowel, and shake once or twice to dislodge from the pan. Turn the right way up and cool on a wire rack.

Meanwhile, make the frosting as instructed on page 156, but stir in the vanilla extract or vanilla bean paste at the same time as the cream cheese.

Once the cake is completely cold, use a spatula to spread the frosting thickly on top.

SERVES 9

⅔ stick butter, plus extra for greasing

½ cup water

⅔ cup dark brown sugar

½ cup molasses

½ cup dark corn syrup

3¾ tbsp preserved stem ginger, finely chopped, plus 1 tbsp of its syrup

2 free-range eggs, lightly beaten

1½ cups self-rising flour

1 tsp ground allspice

1 tsp ground ginger

¼ tsp salt

For the vanilla frosting

½ quantity Cream Cheese Frosting (see page 156)

¼ tsp vanilla extract or vanilla bean paste

Gingerbread grandmas

These little gingerbread cookies sum up our attitude to family: from youngest to oldest, everyone is important. Look out for a gingerbread-lady cutter (with skirt). We like to make our grandmas' hair with white frosting. We have even been known to add little handbags.

Preheat the oven to 360°F. Line 2 cookie sheets with nonstick parchment paper.

Place the flour, ginger, pumpkin pie mix, baking soda, and salt in a large bowl. Add the butter and pulse in a food processor or blend with your fingertips until the mixture resembles bread crumbs.

Put the egg, dark corn syrup, and brown sugar into a separate bowl and beat until blended. Pour into the dry ingredients and mix together until a soft dough forms. Wrap in plastic wrap and chill for 30 minutes.

Roll out the dough on a lightly floured surface to the thickness of about 1/8 in. Using a lady-shaped 4–6-in. cutter, stamp out as many grandmas as you can. Transfer to the prepared cookie sheets and bake for 10–12 minutes, until lightly colored. Let the cookies cool on the sheets.

Once cool, decorate the grandmas using the frosting to draw skirts, hair, and glasses, colored writing frosting to mark out eyes and mouths, and silver balls for buttons.

MAKES 15

2¾ cups all-purpose flour, plus extra for dusting

1 tbsp ground ginger

1 tsp pumpkin pie mix

1 tsp baking soda

¼ tsp fine salt

1 stick cold unsalted butter, cubed

1 free-range egg

4 tbsp dark corn syrup

1 cup light brown sugar

Lemon Frosting (see page 128)

colored writing frosting

edible silver balls

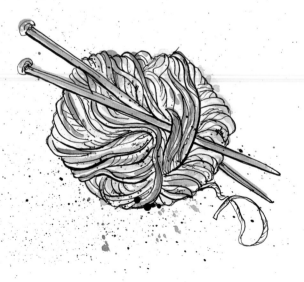

Gluten-free chocolate mud cake

When we first opened our café in Hampstead, north London, baking cakes in our minuscule kitchen was impossible, so we found a wonderful local pastry chef, Alison, to bake them for us. When she moved on to open her own place, we begged her to share a few of her recipes with us in case there was a riot—and luckily, she agreed. We are proud to present her wonderful "mud" cake, which has a soft, mousselike center.

Preheat the oven to 360°F. Grease and line a 9-in. springform cake pan, making sure the paper stands a little higher than the sides.

Put the butter and chocolate into a heatproof bowl set over a saucepan of gently simmering water and allow them to melt.

Meanwhile, separate the eggs into 2 large bowls. Add the cream of tartar to the whites and whisk using an electric hand whisk until soft peaks form. Set aside.

Add the sugar to the egg yolks and whisk until pale, fluffy, and doubled in volume. Pour in the melted chocolate mixture and beat until fully blended.

Sift in the flour and almonds, then fold in using a large metal spoon. When fully combined, gently fold in half the egg whites. When fully incorporated, add the remaining whites and fold in thoroughly. The mixture will be very loose and runny.

Pour the mixture into the prepared pan and bake for 30–35 minutes, until well risen and the top is wobbly just in the center. Carefully remove from the oven and allow it to cool completely and firm up a little in the pan. Transfer to a plate and dust with cocoa powder before serving.

SERVES 8

2¼ sticks unsalted butter, plus extra for greasing

9 oz. dark chocolate (at least 70 percent cocoa solids)

6 free-range eggs

½ tsp cream of tartar

1⅛ cups unrefined superfine sugar

⅓ cup gluten-free self-rising flour

¼ cup ground almonds

cocoa powder, for dusting

Coffee & walnut layer cake

There's something very retro about a triple layer cake. Not only do you get more of the good stuff—the creamy frosting—but it looks impressive, too. Just don't skimp on the espresso. We use our house blend from Bethnal Green's Square Mile Coffee Roasters in London, as we feel it elevates the cake to greatness.

Preheat the oven to 360°F. Grease 3 × 9-in. springform cake pans with butter and line the bases with nonstick parchment paper.

Place the butter in a bowl and beat until pale and fluffy. Add the sugar and beat again until even paler. Add a quarter of the beaten egg and beat at full speed, then add the rest gradually, beating well after each addition. If it curdles, add 2 tablespoons of the flour and beat again.

Add the espresso and mix well. Sift in the flour and baking powder, add the chopped walnuts, and fold together thoroughly.

Divide the mixture equally between the three prepared pans, place them on the middle shelf of the oven, and bake for 12–15 minutes, or until a skewer inserted into the center comes out clean.

Allow the cakes to cool in the pans for 15 minutes, then transfer to a wire rack and peel off the paper. Leave until completely cold.

Meanwhile, make the frosting as instructed on page 156, but stir in the vanilla extract or vanilla bean paste and the espresso at the same time as the cream cheese. Spread it equally on the 3 sponge cakes and sandwich them together. Decorate the top with the chopped walnuts.

SERVES 10

2 sticks soft unsalted butter, plus extra for greasing

1 ⅛ cups superfine sugar

4 free-range eggs, beaten

3 tbsp espresso coffee

1 ¾ cups self-rising flour

1 tsp baking powder

⅔ cup walnuts, finely chopped, plus an extra ¼ cup chopped walnuts, to decorate

For the Frosting

1 quantity Cream Cheese Frosting (see page 156)

½ tsp vanilla extract or vanilla bean paste

2 tbsp espresso coffee

Pantry items

Slow-roasted tomatoes

Roasting tomatoes is a crafty way of getting more flavor out of them when they're not in their peak season. We put them in a low oven with garlic, oil, salt, and pepper and leave them to shrivel, but you need to keep an eye on them. If they release a lot of juice, pour it off or they will boil and disintegrate. On the other hand, you need to catch them before they get too dry. In any event, don't take them off the baking sheet until they have cooled —this will help keep them in one piece.

MAKES 1 LB. 10 OZ.

2 lb. 4 oz. plum tomatoes, cut in half lengthwise

5 garlic cloves

salt and pepper

5 tbsp extra virgin olive oil

Preheat the oven to 285°F.

Place the tomatoes on a baking sheet with the garlic so that they are all snug, season generously, drizzle with 2 tablespoons of the oil, and cook for 2 hours. Check them at regular intervals, as suggested above.

Turn off the oven and leave the tomatoes inside overnight or until the oven has cooled. They should look dehydrated, but not black.

Transfer the tomatoes to a plastic container, cover with the remaining oil, and store in the refrigerator for up to 5 days.

Roasted garlic bell peppers

Bell peppers become so sweet and beautifully silky soft when you roast them—a world away from their crunchy raw beginnings. We throw these into salads and sandwiches with salty cheese and can't get enough of them.

MAKES 9 OZ.

2 red bell peppers
2 yellow bell peppers
6 tbsp olive oil
1 garlic clove, sliced
salt and pepper

Preheat the oven to 425°F.

Place the whole bell peppers in a roasting pan and drizzle with half the oil. Roast for 45–60 minutes, until very soft and the skin has blistered. Transfer to a bowl, cover with plastic wrap, and set aside to cool.

When cool enough to handle, peel off the skins, then core and seed the peppers. Cut into thick slices and place in a plastic container with the garlic. Season well with salt and pepper and cover with the remaining oil. Eat immediately, or store in the refrigerator for 4–5 days. Bring to room temperature before serving.

Caper mayonnaise

This mayo is amazing with most dishes. It goes pretty much with any fish, such as smoked salmon; it's good with salty ham or sliced chorizo (*see* page 105); and it's wonderful with bacon in a chicken bun (*see* page 100).

MAKES 1 CUP

1 tbsp capers

1 tbsp cornichons or homemade pickles

1 cup mayonnaise

1 tsp English mustard powder

juice of ½ lemon

salt and pepper

Rinse and finely chop the capers and cornichons or pickles. Place in a bowl with the mayo, English mustard powder, lemon juice, and seasoning. Mix well, then taste and adjust the seasoning as necessary.

Roasted garlic mayonnaise

Roasting garlic mellows its pungent flavor, so although a whole bulb is used in this recipe, it is nowhere near as strong as raw garlic. We use this mayo in sandwiches, such as our Portobello Mushrooms on Potato Sourdough and Garlic & Fennel Slow-roasted Pork Buns (*see* pages 50 and 96).

MAKES 2 CUPS

1 garlic bulb

pinch of salt

2 cups mayonnaise

Preheat the oven to 400°F.

Wrap the garlic bulb in foil and bake for 40–50 minutes, until really soft when squeezed. Allow it to cool.

When it is cool enough to handle, separate the cloves and squeeze all the soft flesh into a small bowl. Mash with the salt, then stir in the mayonnaise.

Canola oil & English mustard dressing

Our signature dressing includes British cold-pressed canola oil, which gives it a vivid yellow color. With the combination of Dijon and English mustards, we find that it's punchy enough to stand up to strong flavors and perks up milder ingredients, such as lentils and pearl barley.

Combine the salt and mustards in a bowl. Add the vinegar and slowly trickle in the oils, whisking until emulsified. Alternatively, put all the ingredients in a screw-top jar and shake thoroughly rather than whisk.

MAKES 1⅓ CUPS

½ tsp salt

½ tbsp Dijon mustard

1 tsp English mustard powder

5 tbsp white wine vinegar

⅔ cup sunflower oil

½ cup cold-pressed canola oil

Cucumber pickles

Store-bought pickles can be very acidic, so making your own allows you to get the balance of sweetness and acidity just right—and it is also easier than you might imagine. Eat the pickles with braised corned beef (*see* right), smoked salmon, or just a hunk of good cheese and crusty sourdough.

MAKES 3 X 1-QUART JARS

3 cucumbers, sliced ¼ in. thick
1 white onion, thinly sliced
2 tbsp sea salt
½ tsp celery seeds
½ tbsp mustard seeds
1¼ cups white wine vinegar
⅔ cup water
1½ cups superfine sugar

Place the cucumber slices, onion, and salt in a large, nonmetallic bowl and mix well. Cover with plastic wrap and chill for 2 hours. Rinse and drain well, then transfer to a clean bowl.

Sterilize your jars and lids as described on page 30. Pack the cucumbers and onion into the jars so that they fit snugly.

Put the seeds, vinegar, water, and sugar in a small saucepan. Bring to a boil and simmer until the sugar has dissolved. Pour the liquid over the cucumbers so that they are completely covered, topping up with boiling water if necessary. Seal tightly, then label and date. The pickles will keep for at least 6 months.

Braised corned beef

Brisket is our preferred cut for making corned beef. We ask the butcher to salt it for us so that all we have to do is slowly braise it until meltingly tender. We sometimes make a corned-beef hash out of leftovers, frying it with chopped cooked potatoes, softened onions, and a handful of parsley. Otherwise, it's perfect in a sandwich, as on page 102 with pickles.

MAKES 2 LB. 4 OZ.

2 lb. 4 oz. salted beef brisket
1 tbsp black peppercorns
1 tbsp coriander seeds
a few parsley stalks
¾ cup white wine vinegar
1 carrot, sliced
1 white onion, quartered

Soak the brisket in cold water overnight to remove the excess salt, then drain well.

Crush the spices in a mortar and pestle and rub them into the beef. Cover with plastic wrap and leave overnight in the fridge.

Fill a large saucepan with water, add the parsley, vinegar, carrot, and onion, then lower the beef into it and bring to a boil, skimming off any scum that rises to the top. Reduce the heat, cover with a lid, and simmer for 4 hours. Alternatively, place everything in a covered casserole dish and cook in an oven preheated to 285°F for 4 hours.

Slow-braised ham hock

In case you hadn't already guessed, we're passionate about all things porky. We adore a braised ham hock, which has all the texture of a slow-cooked lamb shank but the flavor of a smoky piece of ham. You don't need much of it to perk up a salad or soup, and we love it piled into a sandwich, as on page 99.

Soak the ham hock (also known as pork knuckle) in cold water overnight to remove the excess salt. Drain and rinse well.

Place the hock in a large saucepan with all of the other ingredients and cover with water. Bring to a boil, then reduce the heat, cover, and simmer for 6 hours. Alternatively, place everything in a covered casserole dish and cook in an oven preheated to 285°F for 6 hours.

Allow the hock to cool in the liquid, then drain and peel off and discard the skin. Remove the bone and shred the meat into bite-size pieces. Store in a plastic container and freeze until needed or keep in the refrigerator for up to a week and use as required.

MAKES 1 LB. 2 OZ.

1 lb. 12 oz. smoked ham hock
a few parsley stalks
¼ cup white wine vinegar
1 tbsp black peppercorns
1 carrot, chopped
1 white onion, roughly chopped

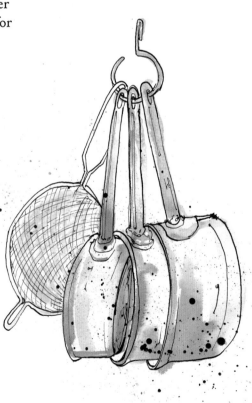

Rosemary sourdough croutons

We go through an enormous amount of sourdough bread in our cafés. Preferring the traditional bloomer shape to the more user-friendly farmhouse loaf, we are often left with lots of little offcuts, where the bread tapers off and is too small to use in sandwiches. Torn and tossed in olive oil, salt, and some fragrant rosemary, these sourdough bits make the most delicious croutons, and they find their way into a lot of our dishes.

Preheat the oven to 360°F.

Place the bread, crusts and all, in a blender or food processor and blitz until you have chunky bread crumbs. Transfer these to a baking sheet.

Crush the garlic into a bowl, then rub with the salt to make a paste. Finely chop the rosemary leaves and stir into the paste along with the oil.

Drizzle the flavored oil over the bread crumbs and mix well. Bake for 25–35 minutes, until golden. The croutons will keep in an airtight container for a week.

MAKES 1 LB.

1 lb. sourdough bread, roughly torn

1 garlic clove

2 tsp sea salt

sprig of rosemary, leaves only

4 tbsp extra virgin olive oil

Cream cheese frosting

If you think you don't like frosting or buttercream, think again. The cream cheese in our recipe adds a sour edge to the mixture to stop it from becoming sickly-sweet. We use this frosting for decorating and filling many of our cakes, such as our Vanilla Cupcakes (*see* page 118), occasionally adding some food coloring or extra flavoring for an alternative. If stored in a lidded plastic container, it will keep in the refrigerator for a week, but allow it to come to room temperature before attempting to spread or pipe it, or you'll find it too stiff.

Put the butter into a bowl and beat until pale and fluffy. Sift in the powdered sugar and beat until smooth, scraping down the sides of the bowl with a spatula to make sure that it is thoroughly combined.

Quickly fold in the cream cheese—don't overbeat or it will become too soft.

MAKES 1 LB. 12 OZ.

2¼ sticks unsalted butter, softened

3¾ cups powdered sugar

½ cup full-fat cream cheese

McIntosh apple sauce

The tangy, juicy sauce we make for our slow-cooked, meltingly tender Garlic & Fennel Slow-roasted Pork Buns (*see* page 96) is made specifically with McIntosh cooking apples. That's because they break down to a beautiful fluffy texture while also retaining the sharpness that makes them so good with rich meats.

Place all the ingredients in a saucepan, cover with a lid and cook over a low heat until the apples have broken down and become fluffy.

Remove the cloves before serving the sauce hot or cold. The sauce can be kept in the refrigerator for 4–5 days.

MAKES 1 LB.

2 lb. 4 oz. McIntosh apples, peeled, cored, and chopped

finely grated zest of 1 lemon

1 ¾ tbsp butter

5 cloves

¼ tsp ground cinnamon

Berry & spice compote

This fruity compote has been draped over our granola and yogurt from the first day we opened our doors in Hampstead. We love the fudgy flavor that the dark brown sugar imparts to it.

Place all the ingredients in a saucepan, cover with a lid, and cook over a low heat until the berries have started to break down but still have some shape. (You don't want something that looks like jam.)

Remove the spices before serving the compote hot or cold. The compote will keep in the refrigerator for 7 days.

MAKES 14 OZ.

1 lb. mixed fresh or frozen berries

3 tbsp dark brown sugar

1 cinnamon stick

2 star anise

Index

ACKNOWLEDGMENTS

Thanks to our loyal customers who support us every day and appreciate the small touches we make for them.

Our staff, who work so tirelessly and passionately, and are like family to us. Our team of chefs: Jess, who was handed the kitchen in Hampstead a week before Tonia had her daughter, Lily, and did wonders with it, and who, along with Scott, our Aussie chef, dreamed up some of these amazing recipes that we still use every day; Shana and Aggie, who have both baked their hearts out in the coldest corner of our kitchen; and Alison, our first-ever baker, who set the incredibly high standard for our cakes.

We give huge thanks to our managers—Henry, Kristina, Adrian, Bosun, and Theres—for their smiles and endless banter. And, of course, to the original Hampstead team—the irreplaceable Hikaru, Josephine, Gaby, Sam, Frearson, and Nick Fahy—without whom none of this would have been possible. To all our baristas, waiters, chefs, and kitchen porters, past and present, who have helped in the creation of Ginger & White, a huge and heartfelt thank you!

Thank you to Alison Starling for being such a G&W fan and visualizing this book from the beginning; to Abi for her incredible illustrations; to Juliette for her designer's eye; and to Jenny Zarins and Tabitha for making the photography so beautiful and for their inability to see any of the food we photographed go in the garbage!

Ginger & White would never have happened if Tonia and Emma's mothers, Diana and Jan, hadn't introduced their two food- and coffee-obsessed daughters to one another, so a massive thanks to our moms. Thanks also to Jamie, Tonia's husband, for his never-ending support, and to Lily, Tonia's daughter, for being there with giggles and cuddles when needed. And, of course, thanks to Alafair and Theo, Emma and Nick's little ones, for their impish grins and for forever keeping us on our toes!